THE NEW PERFORMANCE CHALLENGE

MEASURING OPERATIONS FOR WORLD-CLASS COMPETITION

The BUSINESS ONE IRWIN/APICS Series
in Production Management

Supported by the American Production
and Inventory Control Society

OTHER BOOKS PUBLISHED IN THE BUSINESS ONE IRWIN
SERIES IN PRODUCTION MANAGEMENT

Attaining Manufacturing Excellence   *Robert W. Hall*
Bills of Materials   *Hal Mather*
Production Activity Control   *Steven A. Melnyk and
Phillip L. Carter*
Manufacturing Planning and Control Systems, Second Edition
Thomas E. Vollmann, William Lee Berry, D. Clay Whybark
The Spirit of Manufacturing Excellence   *Ernest Huge*
Strategic Manufacturing: Dynamic New Directions
for the 1990's   *Patricia E. Moody*
Total Quality: An Executive's Guide for the 1990s
The Ernst & Young Quality Improvement Consulting Group

The BUSINESS ONE IRWIN/APICS Series in
Production Management

APICS ADVISORY BOARD
L. James Burlingame
Eliyahu M. Goldratt
Robert W. Hall
Ed Heard
Ernest C. Huge
Henry H. Jordan
George W. Plossl
Richard Schonberger
Thomas E. Vollmann
D. Clay Whybark

THE NEW PERFORMANCE CHALLENGE

MEASURING OPERATIONS FOR WORLD-CLASS COMPETITION

J. Robb Dixon
Alfred J. Nanni, Jr.
Thomas E. Vollmann

BUSINESS ONE IRWIN
Homewood, Illinois   60430

Sponsoring editor: Jim Childs
Project editor: Paula M. Buschman
Production manager: Diane Palmer
Compositor: Compset, Inc.
Typeface: 11/13 Century Schoolbook
Printer: Arcata Graphics/Kingsport

Library of Congress Cataloging-in-Publication Data

Dixon, J. Robb.
   The new performance challenge: measuring operations for world-class competition / J. Robb Dixon, Alfred J. Nanni, Jr., Thomas E. Vollmann.
      p.   cm.—(The Business One Irwin/APICS series in production management)
   ISBN 1-55623-301-9
   1. Performance standards.   2. Industrial productivity— Measurement.   3. Efficiency, Industrial—Evaluation.   I. Nanni, Alfred J.   II. Vollmann, Thomas E.   III. Title.   IV. Series.
HF5549.5.P35D59   1990
658.5′036—dc20

89–48446
CIP

Printed in the United States of America

3 4 5 6 7 8 9 0 K 7 6 5 4 3 2 1 0

To
Barb
Debbie
Tani

PREFACE

"This is your opportunity to challenge the ground rules." William O'Brien, vice president of operations for McNeil Pharmaceutical, gave this charge as his people began to apply the principles and processes described in this book. Their objective was to assess and *to change their performance measurement system* in order to make their organization more competitive.

During the 1980s, American manufacturers applied an alphabet soup of action programs designed to make their manufacturing functions competitive—JIT, SPC, CIM, MRP, and TQC for example. Implementation of these approaches has begun to restore and enhance competitiveness in the manufacturing sector, but the full potential for improvement is far from achieved. Performance measurement has proved to be one of the greatest barriers to successful adoption of these action programs.

In our contacts with executives, we often heard tales of partial success hindered by existing performance measures. Initially this led us to ask, "What is wrong with cost accounting?" When we presented this idea as a research project to Boston University's Manufacturing Roundtable, the members enthusiastically supported it. Yet, as the research progressed, we discovered we were chasing the wrong question. What companies needed was a *process* by which they could continually realign their strategies, actions, and measures, not just a new cost accounting system. Identifying specific fixes for existing cost accounting systems might lead to some marginal improvements, but significant advances were more likely to spring from a different line of inquiry.

The solution to the performance measurement problem lies not in creating some new monolithic system of measurement but in institutionalizing a process for continuously changing measures. Competitive environments vary widely between industries, within industries, and even within companies. The strategies and tactics employed by a market leader in a mature industry will not look the same as those of its followers or as those of a market leader in an embryonic or rapidly growing industry. Why should the measures used to track the effectiveness of those strategies and tactics be the same? Clearly, they should not. Similarly, strategies and tactics change over time. Measures should, too. Managers need to understand when measures support or inhibit desired behaviors and change them accordingly.

The performance measurement questionnaire described in this book is one means by which managers can assess the status of their measurement systems. Our original direction led us to gather data from plants facing a variety of competitive challenges so we could understand the relationships that determine appropriate measures. We concluded that measures need to be unique to particular situations. The focus of our research shifted. We discovered that administering the questionnaire and interpreting the results yields valuable information that provides managers with a useful framework for initiating change in their measurement systems. The goal is to achieve better alignment among the organization's strategies, actions, and measures.

The objectives of this book are similar: to provide a compilation and analysis of a variety of approaches employed by companies to change measures and to offer a framework for guiding the change process. It is not a simple task, nor is it one that will ever truly be complete. Yet, it is essential. The companies that challenge the ground rules of performance measurement are likely to be the ones best able to tune their operations for world class competitiveness.

This book is the result of a research project that began several years ago. We received assistance from many individuals between that starting point and now. We are grateful to all of them, but several deserve special thanks.

The research project was sponsored by a grant from the Boston University Manufacturing Roundtable. Corporate members of the Roundtable at the time this research was conducted were: Agfa Compugraphic, Booz Allen & Hamilton, Digital Equipment Corporation, Eli Lilly & Company, Ernst & Whinney, General Electric, Honeywell Bull, Interlake, Johnson & Johnson, Northern Telecom, Pillsbury, and Sonoco Products Company. We benefited from discussions with all Roundtable member representatives, who made us aware of relevant ideas in their firms.

One representative in particular, however, stands out for his dedication to this research project. Bob Badelt, assistant vice president, manufacturing at Northern Telecom Incorporated, was an active participant throughout the research project. He not only provided insight and helped crystallize our thinking about changing performance measurement, but he also allowed us to perform a complete test of the performance measurement questionnaire in his company.

We want to express our appreciation to Deans George McGurn and Meg Graham of Boston University's School of Management for their encouragement and support of both the Roundtable and, in particular, this project. They were always ready to step in to actively help when needed. Many other people helped us with particular ideas throughout the course of the project. However, one person to whom we owe a very great debt of gratitude is our good friend and colleague, Jeff Miller. As Roundtable Director at the time, he encouraged us as we faced a daunting and ill-defined project. He was with us at every stage of the project, helping evaluate interim results, providing critical feedback on written material, prodding us when it was needed, and organizing and sponsoring a conference on performance measurement when our data collection was complete.

Finally, we wish to express our deepest gratitude to our wives, busy people themselves, for putting up with often excessive demands associated with this project. It is to them that this book is dedicated.

J. Robb Dixon, Boston, Massachusetts
Alfred J. Nanni, Jr., Boston, Massachusetts
Thomas E. Vollmann, Lausanne, Switzerland

CONTENTS

CHAPTER 1

CHANGING PERFORMANCE MEASURES[1]

Performance improvement is critical to the economic well-being of manufacturing companies. Determining how to *measure* performance improvement, however, raises a set of tough problems in today's global marketplace. There are four fundamental reasons why performance measures must be changed in order to support manufacturing practice improvement:

1. Dissatisfaction with traditional measurement systems is growing.

- Cost-based measures are inconsistent with the new emphasis on quality, just-in-time, and using manufacturing as a competitive weapon.
- Outmoded performance measurement systems are impeding the restructuring required to compete in today's global marketplace.
- The measurement demands of the current manufacturing environment exceed the limits of both traditional cost accounting systems and "new, improved" cost accounting systems.

2. Measurement approaches must support ever-increasing excellence.

---

[1]Several key points in this chapter come from the Manufacturing Futures Project of Boston University, which is directed by Jeffrey G. Miller. Two recent publications are: *Manufacturing Strategies* and *Manufacturing Futures Factbook: 1988 North American Manufacturing Survey*. Both are available from the School of Management, Boston University.

- *All* employees should be involved in the drive to implement new ideas more quickly; the objective is total and continual organizational learning.
- Managers need to spend more time taking actions and less time reporting actions.
- Improvement actions must be integrated across functions and across company borders; the focus should be on process flows spanning the "silos" on the organizational chart.

3. Managerial effectiveness is achieved by integrating strategies, actions, and measures.

- Evolution and learning can and must occur on all three dimensions. As strategic objectives are achieved, new ones are formulated; new actions are required to achieve the objectives, and new measures are needed to encourage and monitor those strategic actions. Moreover, obsolete measures must be discarded.
- The driving force for improvement often comes from strategies, but it can and should also come from actions *and* from measures. That is, new measures can lead to both an evolution in actions and changes in strategy.
- North American manufacturing firms have made significant changes in the actions taken to improve effectiveness in recent years; they have been less successful in revising their measurements.

4. A major failure of existing measurement systems is their inability to focus managerial attention on overhead cost and the deployment of overhead personnel.

- Overhead cost is a growing portion of total cost; improvement actions need to focus more on overhead activities than on the other components of manufacturing cost.
- Transactions drive overhead cost. Manufacturing companies cannot afford to deploy highly paid people in routine transaction processing that does not add value to products.

- The distinction between direct work and indirect work is decreasing.
- All workers need to use their brains as well as their hands; one path to excellence is to continually incorporate work performed by staff functions into basic manufacturing jobs.

DISSATISFACTION WITH MEASUREMENT SYSTEMS

Problems with manufacturing performance measurement are increasingly discussed in meetings of accountants, manufacturing managers, information systems specialists, corporate planners, and various academic groups. Performance measurement systems based on traditional cost accounting data simply do not provide the right kind of information to allow a company to remain competitive in today's marketplace. Many of the typical measures generated by cost accounting systems lead managers away from concentrating on what is truly important in manufacturing.

The typical approach to improving performance measurement systems has been to focus on improving the cost accounting system. However, the real question is:

How can firms measure performance in ways that foster competitive improvement?

This is not the same question as, "What's wrong with cost accounting?" Reporting of costs is not the primary issue, performance measurement is. A search for improvement that is limited to changes in the cost accounting system will probably lead to an improved cost accounting system, but not necessarily to improved manufacturing performance! Instead, the search should center on learning how to establish goals for all levels of the organization that are consistent with winning customer orders and achieving ever-increasing levels of excellence in manufacturing.

EVER-INCREASING MANUFACTURING EXCELLENCE

A focus on ever-increasing manufacturing excellence has two important consequences.

> First, manufacturing must be seen as a competitive weapon, one that must be continually honed. Its strategic capabilities and its role in the corporate arsenal need to be well understood and appreciated. Manufacturing strategy must be derived from, supportive of, and integrated with the overall company strategy.

If the introduction of more new products is the perceived key to corporate survival, then goals and measures consistent with the introduction of new products need to be established in manufacturing. On the other hand, if the company game is faster service to customers (for example, just-in-time deliveries), a different set of goals with its own set of measures may be required in manufacturing. In either case, measures that send the message to "minimize costs in this department" are at odds with these goals. The cost-oriented measures call for a nearsighted examination of trees rather than forest, when, in almost any modern manufacturing scenario, the need is for a greater integration across functional "silos" like engineering, marketing, and manufacturing. A strong customer focus must be reflected both in the objectives for manufacturing and in the measures that lead to those objectives.

> The second important consequence of manufacturing excellence is captured in the term *ever increasing*. There is not, and never will be, a stable set of optimal measures in a dynamic, improving manufacturing organization.

This chapter is titled "Changing Performance Measures" rather than "The New Performance Measures" for a reason. It is not only about *why* to change performance measures, but also about the changing nature of performance measurement systems. A good measurement system needs to be continually changed in order to remain effective. As one set of goals or objectives is satisfied, or as the set of measures becomes too gross to detect improvement, a new set needs to be articulated, and the old set needs to be discarded or modified. This means there can never be a set of good performance measures that is stable over time.

Furthermore, a specific set of useful measures will probably not be possible even at a single point in time across factories making similar products within the same company. In the vast majority of cases, the particular problems and opportunities faced in each situation will vary because of unique market characteristics and organizational cultures. Each plant will travel its own path, and changing measures to meet those unique needs will be an integral part of its quest for excellence. This quest for excellence *can* be successful. However, a search for the golden fleece of a universal, accounting-based system of measures is doomed to failure. Even the apparent victor is likely to recognize eventually that he or she has only been fleeced.

STRATEGY, ACTIONS, AND MEASURES

The practice of manufacturing has been undergoing fundamental changes during the 1980s. Global competition is a reality for all manufacturing companies, and new challenges have emerged. It is increasingly difficult to forecast sales, to manage new product development, to implement all of the "three letter cures" (JIT, MRP, TQC, SPC, and so on), and even to evaluate the performance of the manufacturing function itself.

Balancing Strategy, Actions, and Measures

The challenges are being met by addressing three critically interconnected areas for change, as depicted in Figure 1–1. An effective manufacturing organization will have complete congruence along each side of the triangle in Figure 1–1. Logically, the primary decision choice in managing the triangle relates to manufacturing strategy. For example, many companies are recognizing the need for much better levels of quality. For these companies, improvement in output quality has been identified as a strategic objective. Similarly, other companies are now embrac-

FIGURE 1–1
The Strategy, Actions, and Measures Connection

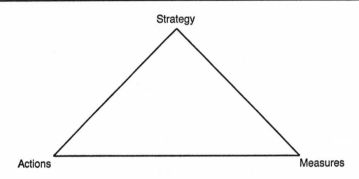

ing time-based competition as a strategy; still others are systematically pursuing greater flexibility in manufacturing.

"Actions" in Figure 1–1 encompass all of the "three letter cures" listed earlier as well as many others. Some of the most popular manufacturing action programs in recent years will be described soon. What is important in the present context is the relationship between actions and strategies. Several alternative action programs always may be undertaken in support of a single strategic objective. Furthermore, although strategies usually come first, actions have led to changes in strategy, too.

A good example of actions leading to strategy can be seen in the evolution of MRP (material requirements planning) into MRP II (manufacturing resource planning). Basic MRP systems were oriented toward improved production and inventory control. MRP II encompasses a game plan for the company, where the strategic directions established by top management are carefully converted into detailed action plans for manufacturing. What this means in terms of Figure 1–1 is that the connection between actions and strategy runs in both directions. Sometimes a change in strategy leads to new actions or programs in manufacturing; other times new improvements in manufacturing highlight the need for changes in the basic manufacturing strategy. What is important is that strategies and actions connect.

The final source of change in manufacturing shown in Figure 1–1 is measures. Many firms are now realizing that outmoded performance measurements inhibit their ability to effectively compete in the marketplace. In the words of one executive:

You get what you measure.

If a company has a strategic objective of achieving better quality, it is not only necessary to have action programs that support quality, but the score-keeping system in manufacturing must also connect to both the strategy and the actions. Performance measures must appraise, reinforce, and reward *improvements* in quality in the terms of the action programs being used to pursue quality.

Emphasis on Learning

Some companies are attempting to improve their manufacturing competitiveness by emphasizing action programs, others are reformulating strategy, while still others are now concentrating attention on developing new performance measures. If care is taken to see that the strategies-actions-measures connections are supported, then starting from any corner of the triangle in Figure 1–1 will eventually lead to the other two. The three directions are complementary and self-reinforcing.

For example, a measurement emphasis on inventory levels might have led an organization to the "discovery" of an action program based on just-in-time (JIT) methods. As the firm became successful with its broad JIT action initiative, there would be reverberations along the connections to strategies and measures. First, management might have noticed it was gaining a competitive advantage because of its ability to get the latest product out the door, built to customer specifications, with very little lead time. This might have led to a recognition that there might be other advantages to having the ability to beat the competition by getting there first, the essence of time-based competition.[2] Thus, a new strategic opportunity may have been identified. Second, moving in the other direction, managers would probably have recognized the JIT methodology was not compat-

---

[2]Time-based competition focuses on the reduction of time as a primary means of competition. Competitive advantage is sought in terms of manufacturing lead times, procurement times, new product introduction (concept to market) times, field service response times, and the entire set of just-in-time concepts.

ible with performance measurement based on traditional labor-based job order costing.

The triangle in Figure 1–1 is meant to reflect the fact that the three directions for improving manufacturing are intimately connected. The relationship between strategy and actions is probably better understood than the relationships between either of them and measures.

> Outmoded performance measurements can seriously impede the restructuring that many manufacturing companies need in order to win customer orders.

One needs to recognize that measures are necessarily tied to strategy; as strategies change, performance measures must change to reflect those new strategies. In a sense, each manager's performance measures should illustrate that manager's role in achieving the strategy. Moreover, strategy and measures are also linked to actions. Improvements in any one can lead to the need for changes in the others, and firms need to learn how to best exploit this relationship. Changing performance measures is not a one-shot fix. No general set of performance measures will apply to every company—or even to the same company over time. Another way of looking at the relationship between strategy, actions, and measures is as a learning process:

> Companies that learn faster than their competitors have little to fear. For learning to be continuous, it must be cultivated through strategies, actions, *and* measures. All three areas, including measures, must evolve over time.

Trends in Strategies and Action Programs

Boston University, through its Manufacturing Roundtable, conducts an annual survey of manufacturing firms. This survey has been conducted for seven years in North America and for six years in Europe and Japan (through associations with INSEAD in France and Waseda University in Japan). The evolution in actions and strategies reflected in this survey is interesting, especially when one considers the behind-the-scenes impact of performance measurement systems.

TABLE 1–1

Comparison of 1984 and 1988 Top 10 Action Programs in North America

1984	1988
Production and inventory control systems	Vendor quality
	Statistical process control
Reducing work force size	Worker safety
Supervisor training	Manufacturing strategy
Direct labor motivation	Worker training
Developing new processes for new products	Integrating information systems in manufacturing
Worker safety	Improving new product introduction capability
Integrating information systems in manufacturing	Integrating information systems across manufacturing and other functions
Reorganization	
Quality circles	
Developing new processes for old products	Manufacturing lead time reduction
	Supervisor training

Source: J. G. Miller and A. V. Roth, *Manufacturing Strategies* (Boston: Boston University Manufacturing Roundtable, 1988).

Several important trends in action programs over the past seven years illustrate the need for changes in performance measures. Table 1–1 shows the top 10 action programs determined in the North American survey in 1984 and the corresponding list for 1988.

Only three action programs are common to both top 10 lists: supervisor training, worker safety, and integration of information systems in manufacturing. Of these, the first two are virtually givens: most firms must continually train people and have ongoing safety programs. This means that only integration of manufacturing information systems has remained over the five-year period out of choice. The inescapable conclusion is that there has been a great deal of change in action programs over the past seven years.

The major change in action programs has been for North American manufacturing firms to get much more serious about quality. In the early years of the survey, quality was a concern.

It was viewed as strategically important, but the primary emphasis in action programs was not quality. As can be seen in the 1984 list, the only quality-related action program was quality circles. This has since become an out-of-fashion fad. North American manufacturers now see the need to focus attention on the kinds of statistically based quality control programs recommended by Demming. That is, *both* the strategy and the actions support quality.

Other significant changes in the list of most popular action programs are the inclusion of manufacturing strategy, the focus on new product introduction, and the reduction of lead time. The underlying themes are a vision of manufacturing playing an equal role to that of the other functions in determining the destiny of the company, the importance of manufacturing in rolling out new products in a shorter time frame, and the thrust of time-based competition:

> Many firms now see the provision of quality products at competitive prices as being the "ante" to play in the game—winning requires a great deal more. New product introductions, product and service enhancements, understanding and solving customer problems, and integrating many staff activities into everyday line activities are the actions that are needed for long-run survival.

This vision implies a manufacturing strategy that reflects these values. More importantly in the present context, it requires a score-keeping system that *tracks progress toward achieving them.*

Another trend from the *Manufacturing Futures Factbook* data that is particularly relevant to performance measurement is a growing interest in better communication of the manufacturing strategy to all levels of the organization. This appears to be particularly important in those cases where the firm sees a need to make fundamental shifts in strategy. Performance measures are major channels of such communication. When measures do not reflect stated new strategies or action programs, the signals are confusing. Furthermore, when the old performance measures square off against the new strategies or actions, the measures often win.

The final trend worth noting is a growing concern with the costs and deployment of overhead personnel. Trends and strategic directions in this area have illustrated the shortcomings of the traditional cost-based performance measurement approach. The impact on performance measurement of this action trend can be seen quite clearly against the backdrop of a comparison between certain North American and Japanese practices.

OVERHEAD COST AND DEPLOYMENT

Figure 1–2 shows the relative distribution of labor for the United States and Japan in terms of the percent of the total manufacturing payroll classified as either direct labor or over-head. As can be seen, there is a significant difference. The direct labor population in the United States receives only about one

FIGURE 1–2
Division of Labor—United States and Japan

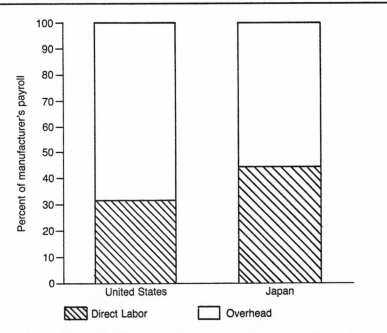

Sources: Miller and Roth, *Report on the 1986 North American Manufacturing Futures Survey*; and Nakane and Amano, *Report on the 1986 Japanese Manufacturing Futures Survey.*

third of the overall payroll, whereas in Japan, the comparable fraction is closer to one half:

> The pay differential between workers and managers is far less in Japan than it is in North America. In Japan, there is less distinction between direct and indirect work.

Job descriptions are less confining; there is work to do and the work force (the *whole* work force) does it. Routine execution is critical, and attention is first devoted to hitting the schedule with flawless quality. Once that objective has been met, however, the attention of *all* workers shifts to improvement: How can the work be done better? What are the roadblocks? How can quality be improved? How can less labor be expended? This change in orientation can also be seen in some North American factories. It is also evident in the recent "lean and mean" movement in North America. Downsizing middle management and removing management layers are typically part of such a process.

The difference in pay differentials is interesting, but what is much more interesting can be seen in Figure 1–3, which shows how the overhead personnel are deployed in the two countries. The ordinate is now stated in the number of direct labor workers per person working in some category of overhead. For example, the first bar is for the number of direct labor workers per manager (Mg), exclusive of first-line supervisors:

> In the United States, there are about 28 direct labor workers per manager, and the comparable number for Japan is 57.

The second set of bars is for first-line supervisors (Sp).

> There are about 14 workers per first-line supervisor in the United States and 8 in Japan. The Japanese have more than 50 percent more first-line supervisors.

A common practice in North America has been to increase this number, leading to a larger span of control. The Japanese seem to believe more first-line supervision makes things work more smoothly. It may also facilitate the changes increasingly required to compete in today's marketplace. When the first two bars are considered together, it can be seen that the Japanese have fewer managers, and they are deployed lower in the orga-

FIGURE 1–3
Staffing Patterns—United States and Japan

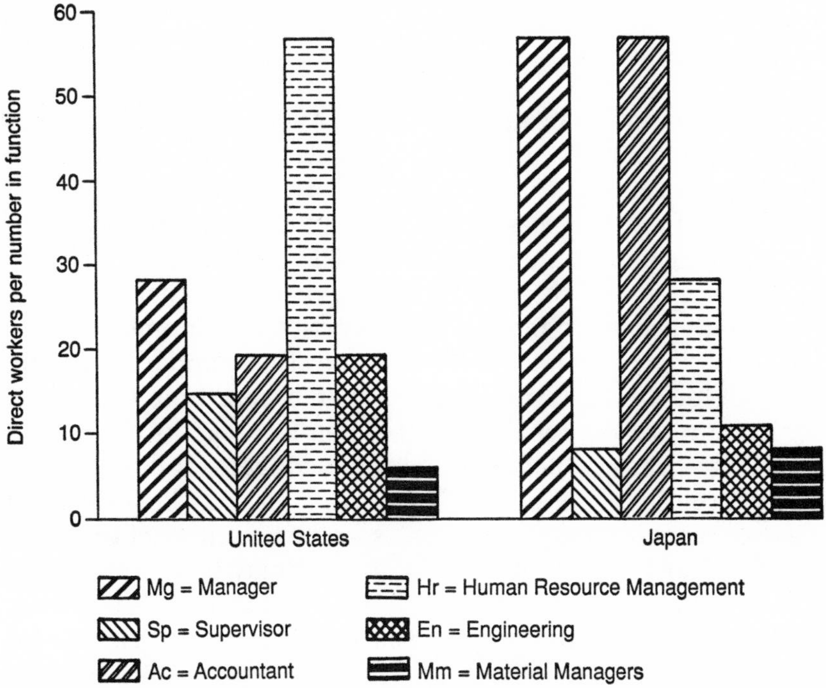

Sources: Miller and Roth, *Report on the 1986 North American Manufacturing Futures Survey* and Nakane and Amano, *Report on the 1986 Japanese Manufacturing Futures Survey.*

nization. This suggests Japanese performance measurement systems are probably less complex and cumbersome than North American systems. There are fewer managers and fewer layers of management to deal with. It also implies that the focus of systems design in Japan must be on communicating strategic activities to the supervisor. There are more of them and there is less between them, in terms of higher management, and the achievement of strategic goals.

The next set of bars is for the number of direct workers per accountant (Ac).

In the United States, we have about 18 or 19 workers per accountant. The comparable number for Japan is 57.

We may have discovered the secret of Japanese accounting: Don't do so much of it! As General Doriot at the Harvard Business School used to say:

Spend your time making it or selling it, not counting it.

The popular notion used to be that the difference in emphasis on accounting was because of all the government regulations in North America. This is unlikely. Americans like numbers. A good part of the business school curriculum is devoted to teaching sophisticated financial analysis. The graduates are good at it. Whether it is either useful or important is another issue. These data suggest a more judicious selection of numbers to report is in order. Taken together with the other comparative data, this may mean managers need to spend more time taking actions and reporting results (what supervisors do) as opposed to reporting actions (which middle-level managers tend to do). The prevalence of accountants in North America may be a result of the excessive overhead positions as well as a source of them.

The fourth set of bars in Figure 1–3 may be the most surprising finding. These bars are for the number of direct labor workers per person in human resource management (Hr): 58 for the United States and about 28 for Japan.

The Japanese have twice as many people working in human resource management.

All those tales of how the Japanese workers get along so well because of common ethnicity, culture, and language may be a smoke screen. They are working at it! Evidence from Japan shows that those human resource people are working on training, recruiting new workers in the high schools, and facilitating change. As new concepts and processes are introduced at an ever faster pace, their job becomes more and more important.

The fifth set of bars is no surprise to most students of manufacturing

The United States has about 19 workers per manufacturing engineer (En), while the Japanese have about 12. The Japanese have 50 percent more industrial engineers.

The last set of bars is for materials managers (Mm). There are about 6 direct workers per person in materials management in the United States and about 8 or 9 in Japan:

> The United States has roughly 50 percent more materials managers than the Japanese.

Another interesting facet of this set of bars is that by being the smallest set, they show the greatest deployment of manufacturing overhead personnel. The greatest source of "hidden factory" is in materials management.[3]

Figure 1–3 does not indicate that *more* managers are employed in the United States. The issue is deployment. What kinds of managers should the company have, and what should they do? How should they spend their time for the greatest overall benefit?

Figures 1–2 and 1–3 considered together imply that the relative pay differential is significantly higher for overhead personnel in the United States, and the ways in which overhead personnel are deployed in the two countries is greatly different:

> Japanese manufacturing overhead people are much less devoted to accounting, to upper management, and to materials management. Instead, their managers are engaged in first-line supervision, in human resource management, and in manufacturing engineering.

This means Japanese managers are more actively involved in making sure things work and in all of the activities that go along with implementing change: people, products, and processes. In short, the overhead personnel appear to be deployed in ways that facilitate learning. Furthermore, such deployment is unlikely to be the product of a performance measurement system predicated on the notion "minimize costs in this depart-

---

[3]The "hidden factory" is that set of activities that pushes numbers into computers and otherwise processes transactions. It can be compared to the "visible factory" that makes widgets. The visible factory gets the greatest attention, but the hidden factory may cost more. Moreover, the real question for the hidden factory is whether it is doing the right things. See "The Hidden Factory," by Miller and Vollmann, in the *Harvard Business Review*, September–October 1985, for more details.

ment." That kind of measurement leads managers to find ways to shift cost burdens outside the department and into the hidden factory.

Recent Changes in Deployment

In the 1988 North American survey, respondents were asked to estimate the percentage changes in 19 categories of manufacturing and nonmanufacturing employees during the prior three years. Figure 1–4 provides the results, revealing a few significant changes. There has been about a 35 percent decrease in the overhead personnel deployed in production planning and inventory control. At the same time, the employment of people in both material handling and purchasing increased roughly 20 percent. This reflects an overall decrease in the category labeled "materials managers" in Figure 1–3. It also may indicate more importance being attached to procurement and to more rapid movement of materials through the factory.

The data also reveal a shift toward a larger number of managers closer to "hands on" in the manufacturing process and away from hidden factory roles. This recent shift reflects a move-

FIGURE 1–4
Changes in Staffing Patterns, 1985–1988 (Change in ratio of functional head count to direct labor head count)

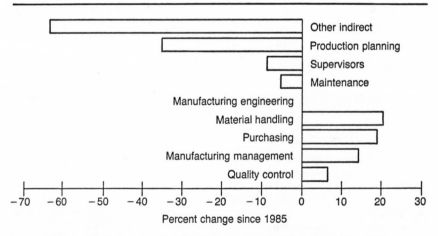

Source: Miller and Roth, *Report on the 1988 North American Manufacturing Futures Survey.*

ment in North American deployment toward something more like that shown in the earlier Japanese data. All of this leads to questions about any changes occurring in the job definitions for direct workers—and the resultant implications for performance measurement.

Knowledge Work

Most of the changes occurring in manufacturing (i.e., the actions) result in changes in the ways people do their jobs. If higher quality products are desired, building the products with the higher quality has to become part of the job in manufacturing. If lead times are to be reduced and time-based competition is to be implemented, the focus of the work force (and of the measurement system) has to shift from worker and machine utilization to material velocity. If new products are to be introduced more quickly with faster achievement of steady state cost/quality results, then the job in manufacturing is again changed—to focus on the new product introduction process instead of on manufacturing in a steady state condition. The job is also changed in engineering—to achieve more new products faster.

What each of these changes in job design implies is a greater degree of knowledge work on the part of the workers:

> The key to manufacturing excellence is in using knowledge workers effectively and in increasing the knowledge work done by all employees.

A company cannot afford to use its overhead personnel (i.e., its knowledge workers) in the processing of large volumes of routine transactions. Nor can it afford to have these higher paid individuals perform the same jobs, day in, day out, with little learning and improvement in their design.

Companies that learn faster than their competitors have little to fear. Learning means new ideas are implemented quickly. Experience with implementation of MRP systems illustrates the problem.

> Virtually every one of the systems whose implementation the authors have witnessed took three or four times as long as planned, cost three times as much as estimated, yielded only 75 percent of

the anticipated benefits, but nonetheless resulted in all parties involved congratulating each other!

Satisfaction at that level is not good enough. The cost overruns are the least of the problems. Much more important is the opportunity cost associated with the personnel (usually the best and the brightest) being tied up in these projects for such a long time. The time of these knowledge workers is the most valuable commodity in the firm for implementing new ideas—that is, for learning.

Many books and articles have been written about Japanese manufacturing systems. Perhaps the *real* secret lies here:

> Japanese manufacturing companies seem to have the ability to implement new ideas faster than their competitors.

For example, a visit by one of the authors to a Japanese electrical firm ended with a plea to the author for any improvement ideas that could be provided. One was offered that would better coordinate engineering and manufacturing for new products, but it involved some major changes in computer systems and organizations. On a return trip one year later, it had all been done!

> The Japanese approach to quality includes the idea that a defect is a gem. This concept goes far beyond the usual notion of a defect. Included are *any* imperfections—particularly imperfections in the underlying support systems for manufacturing.

All companies need to get improvement projects (actions) implemented faster, with less use of scarce knowledge worker time. Also needed are ways for more people to work on such projects, instead of on routine transaction processing. This gives rise to the notion of the "whole person," where the work traditionally done by staff personnel is increasingly made a part of the basic manufacturing infrastructure. This requires measurement systems that support the new directions.

The Whole Person Concept

The "whole person concept" recognizes a need to hire people for their brains as well as their backs. The people who work in manufacturing need to continually improve performance, where improvement is measured on several dimensions consistent with marketplace dictates. More output may be one of these improvements, but definitely included are better quality and the ability to manufacture a greater variety of products and a wider range of volumes.

In many factories, just-in-time concepts will be implemented in nonrepetitive manufacturing environments. The objective will be to operate with very small inventory levels, with customer orders manufactured as required. Enough "whole people" will be employed to produce the varying daily requirements. As learning occurs, a smaller proportion of the working day will be required to complete the manufacturing requirements for the day. When work is not required for daily requirements, the result is employee time available for other activities. Among these activities will be a continuing investment in training, allowing work done by staff support groups, such as quality control and scheduling, to be incorporated into the basic job of manufacturing:

> Under the whole person approach, idle time becomes "brain time"—a resource to be cultivated!

All of this implies fundamental change in the manufacturing culture. The jobs people do will change. Activities normally done by staff specialists will be done as a part of regular production jobs. Overhead personnel will be redeployed and available for application to strategic problem solving. Organizational learning will take place at a faster pace. But the viability of such a future clearly requires institution of a measurement system that is compatible with this kind of growth in job design and one, moreover, that encourages change.

As an example of such a performance measurement system, consider how whole person growth might be measured in a JIT environment. An intriguing measure might develop:

> Increase idle time of the workers on the JIT line.

If schedule and quality performance can be taken as a given, then the line should always attempt to achieve this given in less time, thereby increasing idle time (under the traditional definition). This idle time is thereafter to be used for learning— in whatever ways make the most sense. The learning might be in the use of personal computers to improve scheduling or quality control. It might be in training to achieve more flexibility in worker assignments. It might be in supervisory techniques to more easily integrate temporary employees. It might be in some task now done by a staff function to increase *their* idle time so *they* can learn something important.

The concept of maximizing idle time is fundamentally different from the usual controls applied to manufacturing. It implies a major shift in the philosophy and culture of most firms. It recognizes that work is more than simply lifting boxes, turning bolts, or pushing buttons. It is an idea directly at odds with performance measurement based on traditional cost-based metrics, which recognizes only those physical activities. It is *not*, however, an impossibility. Once the other appropriate performance measures are in place, it can be done. In fact, two of the authors have visited a plant in which this sort of thing was being planned. The manager involved said it would bring training out from "below the [cost and budget] books."

This brings us full circle to the issue of the role of cost accounting systems in performance measurement. As indicated at the beginning of this chapter, the idea that a traditional (or even a new) standard cost accounting system can provide one all-embracing system for performance measurement problems is ill-conceived. This conclusion was not jumped on simply in reaction to a frustration with traditional accounting-based measures. On the contrary, accounting needs to play an important role in manufacturing organizations; that role is rapidly changing, and the accountants need to help in focusing the change process. The conclusion that it should not be the fulcrum of a performance measurement system is drawn from observation of firms wrestling with the performance measurement issue, some successfully, some not. Such frustration with accounting-based measures *does* seem to be the general point of awakening to performance measurement concerns for most organizations and represents the typical setting for the metamorphosis called the three phases of change. This is the subject of the next chapter.

CHAPTER 2

THE THREE PHASES OF
CHANGE

Barbara Friesner, manager of service part sales for Amalgamated Machines, was wincing. Profitability on service parts had decreased again last year, even after prices had been increased by 20 percent. "I just don't understand it; it takes no more labor hours to make these parts than it ever did, the union only got a 5 percent increase in wages, the equipment is fully depreciated, and our material costs have actually decreased. We must be using the wrong yardstick to evaluate this product line."

Does this sound like a familiar complaint? Many firms encounter similar experiences with measures, even in the successful pursuit of changing their performance measurement systems. The "Three Phases of Change" identifies stages companies are likely to pass through after reaching the level of frustration with traditional cost-based performance measures exhibited at Amalgamated Machines. The three phases are:

1. *Tinkering with the cost accounting system.* Clinging to the notion that the cost accounting system should be the major source of performance measurement, many companies focus their attention on the inadequacies of the costing system and spend inordinate amounts of time, money, and effort trying to make the performance measurement system work by "fixing" the cost accounting system.

2. *Cutting the Gordian Knot.* According to legend, in ancient times King Gordius of Phrygia tied a massive knot on the yoke of his chariot. An oracle declared that whoever loosed the Gordian Knot would rule the world! Many challengers tried to untie the knot, but failed. Alexander the Great simply drew his sword and cut the knot in two! A few companies, finding that even great amounts of tinkering *still* left them with inadequate performance measurement, have similarly discovered that the simple, bold move of cutting the knot between accounting and performance measurement is much more effective than trying to untie it.

3. *Embracing change in strategies, actions, and measures.* Once performance measurement is unbound from accounting, an organization's focus can be directed toward making adaptive, preemptive change a matter of course. Getting there first and better is the way to rule the competitive world. However, reaching the point where the organization can embrace change usually requires a massive turnaround in attitudes and behavior.

This framework reflects observations of manufacturing companies making successful advances in changing their performance measures. The three-phase framework represents a distillation of these observations, some of which will be detailed in later chapters. The framework is offered in the hopes that other companies can use it to assess their own stage of progress toward the goal and to help themselves reach that goal.

The Setting for Change: Frustration with Accounting-Based Systems

Evidence from the *Manufacturing Futures* survey and from discussions with manufacturing executives shows a growing frustration with the inadequacies of traditional cost-based performance measures.

> As quality and time become critical to company survival, measures that are driven by quarterly earnings reports and investment decisions that are based solely on "cost savings" are less and less relevant to promoting long-term company health.

According to a recent survey of manufacturing companies co-sponsored by the National Association of Accountants (NAA) and Computer-Aided Manufacturing—International (CAM-I), 60 percent of the executives polled expressed dissatisfaction with their firms' performance measurement systems. In the electronics industry, where both manufacturing and market environments have changed most, 80 percent were dissatisfied.[1]

> Traditional measurement of direct laborers on the shop floor has become increasingly less relevant to the attainment of corporate objectives.

The factory must routinely execute on schedule, with high quality and low cost. The routine things need to be done routinely, with more knowledge work done by all employees, both direct and indirect workers. But the changes required to restructure manufacturing operations for global competition are inhibited by the inappropriate use of traditional financial measures and accounting controls.

Traditional cost accounting systems are built on the premise that direct labor is a major source of value added; this is no longer true for most companies. Furthermore, by applying overhead on a direct labor basis, these systems imply that full utilization of labor will lead to efficient manufacturing. This practice is likely to lead, instead, to the creation of unwanted and unnecessary inventories. The result is a more costly operation than one that makes products only in response to actual customer needs. Overhead for carrying inventory, including personnel, facilities, and financing costs, simply add to the allocations, encouraging units to make even more product.

Just-in-time methods clearly expose the fallacy of building inventories. The concept of "material velocity" (increasing the speed with which materials flow through a factory) is now being viewed as a competitive weapon. Initially used only in repetitive manufacturing environments, JIT is now being applied in nonrepetitive manufacturing environments where surges in volume are readily accommodated.

A JIT company near Boston can achieve a 300 percent increase in volume in six weeks (the time to get materials) with no addition of permanent employees. Each worker has learned

---

[1]Robert A. Howell et al., *Management Accounting in the New Manufacturing Environment* (Montvale, N.J.: National Association of Accountants, 1987).

to train temporary workers and to act as their supervisor. This allows the permanent employees to have great job security and the company to be responsive to the dictates of the market. This company makes CAD/CAM/CAE terminals. Before implementing JIT, products had a 15-to-20-week manufacturing lead time, manufacturing ran with a steady rate of output, and the company produced for finished goods. The firm now produces products in four days, only for specific customer orders, and is able to increase or decrease volume levels significantly within the six-week window. This company has also achieved major savings in obsolete materials, manufacturing planning and control personnel, and floor space.

> After all these things (and many others) were accomplished, a controller from the corporate office went on a tour of the factory. Not seeing the usual flurry and din he had come to associate with "work getting done," he immediately assumed that productivity was low. He recommended that the company implement a standard cost accounting system!

The manager in charge of this JIT implementation asked for aid in helping to explain the situation. He knew a standard cost system would measure all the wrong things and wreak havoc with the new, finely tuned manufacturing system.

The qualities that made this operation function so well were the enemies of traditional budget variances. Labor and overhead efficiency measures would push managers away from employee training and toward the buildup of inventory. Rate variances would indicate that production was cheapest when the lowest paid (temporary) were in use. This would encourage either high volumes (with the associated inventory buildup) or high employee turnover (with an associated loss in volume flexibility). All this would happen despite the fact that bottom-line measures had already shown the current approach to be more efficient than the traditional approach!

Many such "war" stories exist. The key points are:

* Managers are frustrated with traditional cost-based measurement systems.
* The strategic importance of cost is shrinking in comparison to the newer strategic objectives in manufacturing.

- Cost is an accounting convention subject to wide latitude.
- Cost is best seen as a passenger, just along for the ride. Other factors drive costs.
- Managers who treat cost and short-term financial measures as drivers may be sacrificing long-run company health.

As companies become aware of the shortcomings of using their traditional cost accounting systems for performance measurement, they tend to view the problem as in the cost accounting system itself. This, however, is false. Many of the performance measurement problems described above are caused by the misuse or misapplication of cost-based data. It is not that the data are incorrect so much as it is that the data are being used for purposes they can never satisfy.

The plain fact is that cost accounting data are insufficient for the performance measurement task. Cost data are not necessarily irrelevant. Later chapters will show that accounting-based performance measures have useful information, even in very modern manufacturing environments. However, accounting measures of performance are useful only when they are appropriately balanced with nonfinancial measures of performance, when the scope of the performance activities to which they are applied is reduced, and, most critically, when managers use them in a more enlightened, less knee-jerk way.

This last issue, a behavioral one, is probably a major reason companies tinker with their cost accounting systems in reaction to performance measurement problems. First, many of the accounting systems are less than what they could be. There are accounting-specific problems due to a misapplication or overapplication of accounting concepts. These problems are simply ones of poor system design, not flawed accounting concepts or poor system implementation. Furthermore, old cost accounting systems represent a set of bad managerial habits. It is easy for managers to be seduced into believing that, if they just learn good accounting habits, everything will be fine. Thus, it is easy to find examples of firms in the first phase of the three-phase framework. Managers must remember, though, that shining their shoes will not cause them to walk faster.

PHASE ONE—TINKERING WITH COST SYSTEMS

The first phase of development in changing measures of performance in manufacturing is to modify or tinker with present cost-based systems in order to "better reflect reality." The typical approach is to attempt new methods for overhead allocation. Many firms have decided that because a growing proportion of their product cost is from purchased materials, they should allocate all overhead costs associated with purchases to these items. While this may appear to be a laudatory idea, it has some basic flaws. For example, assume overhead is allocated on the basis of purchasing costs. What happens when there are two product lines, one mature and the other new with many engineering changes? Do they both require the same degree of attention from purchasing managers? from engineers? from quality control?

The traditional labor-based allocation of overhead is often cited as a source of performance measurement problems. Such a problem occurred at a firm similar to Amalgamated Machines. All of the new products were designed for manufacture on the latest numerical controlled equipment. The older items, especially spare parts, continued to be made on the manual machines and had longer setup times. Because products were charged at a rate based on labor hours, the old items looked like losers. They took longer to make so they absorbed more overhead per unit. Moreover, the overhead they had to absorb was high because of the depreciation charges from the new equipment, equipment used to make other products! This firm concluded performance measurement was inadequate because the cost accounting system employed poor overhead application techniques. Consultants were brought in to design a system to more fairly allocate overhead.

> Administrative overhead was increased by the cost of the study and factory overhead by the cost of the new systems, but production was not improved. No problem was eliminated, just the false perception of a problem. No efficiencies were gained in manufacturing, no new value was provided to the customers, and the bottom line was reduced.

Perhaps the famous line by Bosquet (on the charge of the Light Brigade at Balaklava), "It is magnificent, but it is not war," should be altered to describe such work: It is magnificent, but it is not competitive!

> Tinkering with cost accounting does not make performance measurement better, just less annoying. Tinkering with cost accounting makes the cost accounting system better. It does not fix problems of performance improvement that cannot be directly reflected in cost accounting data.

Goldratt and Cox, in their classic, *The Goal,* make the point that an hour of capacity lost at a bottleneck work center is an hour of capacity lost to the entire factory, and therefore extraordinarily costly; while an hour of capacity gained in a nonbottleneck is an illusion that will unnecessarily increase work-in-process inventory.[2]

> Traditional cost accounting-based performance measurement systems that misdirect managers' attention and encourage full utilization of workers and equipment in making products are actually the enemy of productivity.

Some people suggest managers can be made to "think right" through the cost accounting system if the cost accounting system could be redesigned to reflect the true sources of costs. However, the sources of costs in a modern manufacturing concern are Byzantine in their complexity. A system that reflected those sources would be equally complex. In some situations, where careful cost analysis is the critical issue, this level of complexity is appropriate. But such complexity would not lead to a practical performance measurement system, which must communicate performance criteria in a way that can be simply and clearly translated into goal-congruent actions.

It is useful to identify three separate objectives for which cost accounting data are used.[3] The first is financial reporting

---

[2]E. M. Goldratt and J. Cox, *The Goal* (Croton-on-Hudson, N.Y.: North River Press, 1984).

[3]See also A. J. Nanni, J. G. Miller, and T. E. Vollmann, "What Shall We Account For?" *Management Accounting,* January 1988.

with the objective of reporting financial health of the enterprise to outside interests such as shareholders and creditors. The second activity for which cost accounting data are used can be called *cost modeling*. Cost data are used for pricing studies, for analysis of product line profitability, for one-time decisions, and for make-buy analysis; in short, for planning. The third use for cost accounting data is feedback and control, the area that includes performance measurement. This has usually been accomplished with variance reporting and similar approaches.

Separation of accounting into these three categories leads to some useful observations. There will always be a need for category one, and the present methods of costing for reporting to outside interests are probably as good as any (they are not broken, so don't fix them). The problems occur in categories two and three. In both cases, traditional cost accounting-based performance measurement systems can easily lead to poor decision making. Moreover, tinkering with existing approaches simply will not do the job. As long as the category one requirement exists that the results of cost accounting add "up and down," from total factory cost to unit product cost to cost of goods sold to ultimate external reporting, the results will be problematical.

> Each planning decision should rest on whatever basis makes the most sense for that problem. A cost modeling approach implies that the choice criterion is simple cost reduction or short-term profit increment. There are many long-term decisions, such as investments in new technology, that cannot be based on simple cost reduction. The real question is what will happen if the firm does not make the investment? There are short-horizon and one-time decisions that are similarly situation dependent. No amount of tinkering with accounting systems will solve this problem.

A food products company illustrates the point. This company built two new factories even though the capacity was not required. The decision was a strategic one, to put the "bread and butter" production into new, highly focused factories, so the main plant could concentrate on new product introductions. The firm believed the key to long-run success was to bring out twice as many new products each year. This would simply not be possible if the present factory also had to push out high-volume products. The measures used to evaluate the three factories clearly had to be changed. The older main plant has a different competitive charter and has to be measured against new product rollout objectives. The two new plants are evaluated in more traditional ways: cost, quality, schedule performance, and learning curve measures.

The investment decision was predicated on a belief that profitability would be improved in the future as compared to a future without such an approach. However, with no history of double-rate product introduction as a market factor, historical cost was of limited value. Furthermore, the benefits of the decision were easily seen in terms of strategy but not so easily viewed in terms of hard dollars. Finally, once the main plant had been reoriented toward new product introduction, traditional cost-based measures would have led manufacturing managers in the wrong direction; short-term departmental cost minimization would have discouraged experimentation and learning and, thus, lengthened the development time, the critical factor.

> The use of a cost accounting-based system to achieve the third traditional objective, feedback and control, is even more problematical. First, as shown above, periodic departmental costs may not be the appropriate criterion against which to measure progress. Second, even if such costs represent a critical outcome, the cost-based signals are not "real time." For most firms, by the time accounting-based variances are determined, it is far too late to do anything about the problems. Third, and finally, the suggested cure may not match the disease. Cost variances are passengers, not drivers. Controlling against such signals may lead managers to manage the symptoms, not treat the disease.

The right feedback on performance drivers has to be presented in real time and in action-oriented terms; that is, quality control has to be current and specific.

> For most critical manufacturing variables, the idea of waiting until a week after month's end to determine overall performance is ridiculous!

It is input and process variables that need to be controlled. Outcomes, like cost, can only be controlled through those inputs and processes. If input and process variables are held in tight control, the financial results should work out. If they do not, the fault lies in one of three areas: the strategy, the actions chosen to implement the strategy, or in the financial analysis itself.

Far too many situations exist where, because of the message implicit in the cost-based performance measures, costs have been viewed as drivers to the overall detriment of the company. Examples include building unneeded inventories to utilize capacity and "improve" manufacturing variance measures, restricting capital expenditures to make return on investment look better, and forgoing important maintenance projects.

Another reason the cure may not match the disease relates to the evolution of feedback and control reporting.

> As performance improves, new measures and new controls are appropriate.

Similarly, when performance slips for some reason, the required level of analysis may easily change. For example, when some products are not up to the desired quality levels, analysis might lead to some area of the factory that needs to be tightly controlled with statistical process control. Later, when the processes can be run with no problems, perhaps the level and degree of control can be relaxed. But, if an unexpected problem occurs, some new highly focused feedback and control mechanisms may be needed. The key point here is one of contingency:

> Conditions define the problems and problems define the feedback mechanisms.

The use of performance measurement systems built entirely within cost accounting systems runs counter to this notion. There, the same set of measures is collected at all times, irrespective of current problem definitions. Granted, cost-based systems *can* be made a bit more flexible. That is what tinkering is about. However, in the end, the nature of accounting control makes it unlikely that frequent changes can be made in the system of measures or that changes can be made by, for example, individual work cell supervisors.

The three activities traditionally performed by a cost accounting system can be viewed in terms of the timing, the scope, and the demand for the activity. This view reinforces the conclusion that there is a basic incompatibility that cannot be satisfied in one monolithic system.

In financial reporting, the timing for the process is periodic; there are monthly, quarterly, and annual cycles for reporting the financial position of the company to outside interests. Cost modeling, on the other hand, tends to be more ad hoc, based on events and opportunities. Feedback and control need to be done on a continuous basis.

Financial reporting requires exhaustive, aggregate data, which, as a result, do not vary from period to period in terms of scope. For both cost modeling and performance measurement, the case is just the opposite. The scope of the relevant data is dictated by the nature of the decision at hand or the process being controlled and thus will vary from case to case. Furthermore, the nature of the data to be included will differ between cost modeling and performance measurement.

The primary source of demand for financial reporting comes from outside interests, investors and creditors, and is channeled through regulatory bodies such as taxation authorities, the Securities and Exchange Commission, and the public accounting profession. The demand for cost modeling, on the other hand, is tactical or strategic. It is based upon an analysis of opportunities in the marketplace matched with capabilities in the company. In the area of feedback and control, the demand seems to be drawn from strategies and action plans, mediated by operating conditions and stability. The primary efforts are to drive out variability and make operations completely predictable in terms of strategic characteristics like quality and schedule performance.

> The overall implication is that the three activities commonly associated with cost accounting are fundamentally incompatible. The problems caused by this incompatibility are growing at a fast pace, fed by the challenges of the marketplace and new approaches to manufacturing.

International competition demands that companies adopt situation-dependent performance measures focused on long-run economic well-being, not short-run expediency and outdated concepts. The emphasis has to be on managing resources, not managing costs, and on deploying resources—particularly human resources.

Performance measurement systems, in and of themselves, *do not add value* in manufacturing. Cost-based systems often misdirect attention. They ignore large strategic issues. Tinkering requires the creation of large, more complex cost accounting systems. These systems are difficult to change in reaction to changes in actions or in response to learning. What is the point of straining to create expensive, inadequate cost accounting systems for performance measurement when simpler, more direct approaches are possible?

PHASE TWO—CUTTING THE GORDIAN KNOT

Some firms have concluded there simply is no way a cost accounting system can or should be used for all three activities. It will always be necessary to report to outside interests on a basis consistent with that of other firms. But there is no reason to similarly constrain either cost modeling or feedback/control. In both of these activities, the firm should base its actions on whatever best matches its set of strategic objectives.

> Cutting the Gordian Knot requires a conscious decision by top management to no longer match internal reporting to the dictates of external reporting. Saying this and actually replacing cost accounting in these latter two functions are two very different things. Many people will agree with the basic notion, but will they be able to make the change? Will they cut the Gordian Knot that ties short-term financial accounting to decision making in manufacturing? Will they not only adopt new performance measurements, but also discard those that are no longer appropriate? What sort of change process needs to occur in a company for this to happen?

One electronics firm recently gave up absorption costing for all internal reporting. By itself, the new alternative (direct costing) is not a panacea. However, it is no longer possible in this company to increase profits by building inventory. The change provoked a new awareness as to what was truly important in manufacturing. Accompanying this change in accounting was the participative development of a well-defined manufacturing strategy for the company. This strategy clearly defined objectives for manufacturing in terms of revenue growth, overhead growth, inventory (material velocity), quality, and new product introductions. The strategic objectives led to a definition of what was important to measure, and the abandonment of absorption costing provided a way to unshackle the old measurement constraints.

A similar knot cutting has been done by a computer manufacturer. This company has given up standard capital appropriation approaches for a large portion of the budget for improving manufacturing processes. Instead, the firm has allocated funds for what it calls *manufacturing research and development*. This allocation is to be used to support projects that can be proposed from anywhere in the company. The firm has a standard format for proposals, and it has published guidelines for what is and is not to be considered manufacturing R&D. The proposals are sorted into categories (called *bins*), and each has a bin manager assigned to coordinate and evaluate progress. The size of the appropriation has grown by approximately 50 percent per year over the past nine years. The most interesting aspect in this example of Gordian Knot cutting is that the selection process for projects is not based on the usual financially driven criteria. The primary question is the potential for enhancing the products and services offered to customers. Cost payback or return on investment are not part of the evaluation process.[4]

Another Gordian Knot cutting example is the growing tendency among high-tech companies to abandon the concept of direct labor. These firms increasingly view their employees as an asset to be managed and enhanced. They employ people, not direct and indirect workers. There is work to do, and there will be continual redefinition of who is to do what. The objective is to evolve as quickly as possible (that is, to learn). Employees need to continually increase their skill base and take on new challenges.

---

[4]See F. D. Cassidy and T. E. Vollmann, "Enhancing Manufacturing Processes," Working Paper, Boston University Manufacturing Roundtable, 1987.

The abandonment of direct labor as an activity basis means accounting necessarily needs to change the basis for many kinds of calculations.

It is not enough to say the category is abandoned and then to measure labor hours under another name (which a few companies have done). Costs of products clearly cannot be determined in the same way. This forces people to think less about cost and more about the nature of decisions. For example, the focus might shift from some parochial view of product cost to a better understanding of where the knowledge workers of the company are being deployed and whether this is the best use of their time.

The approach to cost accounting called *activity-based accounting* or *transaction accounting* involves this kind of examination of cost drivers. The adoption of transaction accounting, however, does not constitute Gordian Knot cutting, although it may be part of such an action. The crux of cutting the Gordian Knot is simply giving the cost accounting system and the performance measurement system separate identities!

A key issue in Gordian Knot cutting is *who is going to participate in the change process?* Experience indicates it is critical for the financial function to buy in. Manufacturing cannot do it alone, and financial people need to understand that they have to be a part of the solution instead of being only a part of the problem. Without this commitment, the company would not be expected to get beyond the grousing stage. In the United States, the financial function has significant power in most companies. They can provide the necessary clout to make changes, or they can block the changes.

Another critical component of the Gordian Knot cutting is *a well-articulated manufacturing strategy*. When this is in place, the firm becomes committed to achieving a set of marketplace objectives, and manufacturing is seen as playing a central role in the achievement of those objectives. The result is an agreed upon mission for each manufacturing unit; this more easily leads to a redefinition of what is important, not so important, and what should be measured.

Gordian Knot cutting is essential to making real changes in manufacturing performance measurements. The company needs to understand that tinkering with existing cost accounting-based systems simply will not yield the desired results. It is necessary to release performance measurement from the shackles that are inherent in these systems. Situation-dependent measures need to be established and allowed to evolve as conditions (and strategies) change.

Carried to its logical conclusion, Gordian Knot cutting means the *firm will give up the usual concept of unit product costs* as the concept has been applied in performance measurement. This may sound heretical, but it is fundamental to the act of separating cost measurement from performance measurement. Unit product cost is and has always been an accounting convention. When applied to the overall company on an annual basis, or to product families or strategic business units, the idea of cost makes sense. When applied to inventory valuation for the balance sheet, unit product cost is simply an average, an estimate, a building block for calculating total inventory value. When applied to specific product units in short time frames, the idea does not make sense.

In performance evaluation, unit product cost can add confusion to important decisions. Traditional calculations of unit product costs require overhead allocations that are so arbitrary as to be meaningless. Several examples of this phenomenon appeared earlier in this chapter, such as material cost-based overheads for products at different stages of the product life cycle.

Many people are attempting to construct better models for determining product costs. Most of these approaches require multiple allocations of overheads via several layers of cost pools. They begin by trying to establish an understanding of how costs accumulate, a praiseworthy goal. However, allocating these costs down to the unit level wipes away any good that might have come from the analysis.

> The control actions are still far removed from the measures, but now the measures are claimed to have greater accuracy!

Perhaps only part of the overhead costs should be allocated down. But, even if this is done, the message it conveys may be overly complex for human consumption. Besides, if the correct bases can be identified, why cannot those count figures be used directly in performance measurement? At the very least, this would eliminate the need for a manager to "unpack" the dollar figures.

There is something liberating in saying that unit product costs are meaningless for performance measurement. Perhaps one might want to determine how the time of a set of people is allocated among a few product lines and thereafter determine whether the product line appears to be more or less profitable compared to other lines.[5] But the idea of saying that a particular batch of some product has an exact cost (and therefore profit) is meaningless, and should be so labeled. The result can only be better understanding of what is truly important for the long-run health of the company.

Cutting the Gordian Knot is the first step toward finding truly effective measures of performance. It involves several bold actions:

- It requires the establishment of a well-specified manufacturing strategy.
- It requires the finance and control functions in the organization to accept the idea of nonfinancial performance measures.
- Ultimately, it means abandoning the notion of performance measures based on unit product cost.

PHASE THREE—EMBRACING CHANGE

The final phase in our framework for changing manufacturing performance measures is reached when a firm considers the process of performance measurement as an integral aspect of implementing manufacturing strategy. That is, if strategic goals are to be developed and achieved, it is critical to create performance measures that are supportive of these objectives and to get rid of any measures that are counterproductive. Moreover, as goals are attained and new ones formulated, the performance measurement system should similarly evolve.

---

[5]See Nanni, Miller, and Vollmann, "What Shall We Account For?" for more details on how this might be done.

In fact, perhaps the first thing one should do to implement a change in strategic direction is to consider what changes in performance measures might be most conducive to achieving the change.

Changes in performance measures need to be seen as both top-down and bottom-up efforts. Senior management, through an articulated strategy, should determine the firm's overall direction, but the ways in which the resultant goals are to be achieved and the best ways to support them in particular organizational units are situation-dependent. The companies most successful in institutionalizing change in performance measurement have all used a combination of top-down and bottom-up approaches. At the top, strategy has been formulated, general policies stated, and a few "stretch" objectives declared. From the bottom, specific measures have been formulated, and they have evolved—both as progress was made and as the imperfections of the measures were identified.

Embracing change also implies *changes to organizational structures*. A top-down objective to reduce the time to introduce new products might lead to different programs in particular parts of the company. In one firm, achieving this objective required a combining of design and industrial engineering.

A new culture of cooperation was required, and new career progression steps were initiated.

In another firm, the speeding of new product introduction emphasized bringing new products into production with as few subsequent modifications as possible. This required getting rid of a performance measure for cost reductions. There had previously been a cost reduction budget for manufacturing engineering. Every year, manufacturing engineering was evaluated on how much money was "saved" through redesign of the products and processes. Unfortunately, this led to products being poorly designed in the first place. The new emphasis was on achieving mature cost, which was defined as 110 percent of final cost, within six months of the start of manufacturing. Instead of a cost savings being treated as something good, it was now considered to be a design error if the technology in the improvement had been available at the time of product design.

This example illustrates both a new set of performance measures and elimination of an old set. Both of these are important in phase three. The overall goal is to speed the learning process, to achieve ever more improvements in manufacturing effectiveness faster. This means a performance measure will have importance only as long as it drives manufacturing to achieve new levels of effectiveness. In theory, any measure should be discarded when another will do a better job. The problem is that an organization can absorb directional change only at a limited rate. Establishing the means for working both top down and bottom up can help in speeding the evolution in performance measures.

Eliminating performance measures can be as useful as adding them. In this age of cheap computational power, it is tempting to add more and more measures, without discarding any. Thus, some people will suggest that traditional cost measures be kept and that new measures be added. A good lesson can be learned from the service industries. At the fast-food chains such as McDonald's, the primary measure is simply volume per time period expressed in dollars. The restaurants work with such a high material velocity that there is little point in keeping track of any inventories. The output is in essence the input as well. As manufacturing firms move to JIT the same ideas are true. If quality can be guaranteed and high material velocity achieved, many standard measures can be eliminated.

> Manufacturing's job is to take any order and fill it in a lead time that appears as if the products were held in stock, when in fact little or no finished goods are held.

It is useful to distinguish between strategic measures and maintenance measures. The former set should contain from 5 to 15 measures for a particular organizational unit that reflects its set of strategic goals—the realization of which best indicates learning for this unit. These measures would be set participatively to support some top-down goal. As one or more of these goals are attained, the accompanying measures need to reflect this achievement. Typically, a set of measures can now be collapsed into a more highly aggregated measure, one that can be made less frequently. That is, the measures evolve from the strategic category into the maintenance category. This allows this organizational unit to now take on new goals—and new strategic measures.

Phase three is called *embracing change* because the expectation is that performance measures should be continually improved. Manufacturing excellence is the objective, and the definition of excellence is clearly contingent upon what is being achieved *now*, what the challenges from competitors are *now*, what the best benchmark in any activity in any company (not just a competitor) is *now*, what the new technologies and their associated opportunities are *now*, and what new ideas for enhancing the products and services provided to customers are available *now*.

Using benchmarks is an important activity in many companies that are changing performance measures. The process needs to be done carefully, however. There is a temptation to use existing competitors as benchmarks, asking are we as good as the best of our competitors in service, quality, dependability, or whatever. This is dangerous. Just because one's present competitors are not a threat does not mean this happy state will continue. In today's international competition, a new competitor can come from nowhere, in a hurry. The questions for benchmarks should be based on whoever is the best at the activity—in any industry, in any country. Achieving this degree of excellence should be seen as a strategic objective, as a barrier to entry for competition. Staying ahead is best achieved by continually getting better.

> The major question at a manufacturing strategy session for a capital goods manufacturer was how to keep its market leadership, how to construct greater barriers to entry, and what kind of preemptive manufacturing moves should be made. In this industry, 12-to-20-week deliveries were the norm. The company decided that if it could provide 3-to-4-week delivery on 80 percent of the product line, it would be exceedingly difficult for anyone to compete with it. This goal became the driver for manufacturing changes, both in the manufacturing processes and in the appropriate measurements for manufacturing.

This example illustrates that manufacturing excellence will be achieved through a series of routine actions and projects, directed by an overriding manufacturing strategy and a consistent set of performance measures. The measurement of performance in day-to-day activities and one-time projects needs to be consistent with continually refined, situation-dependent definitions of excellence.

THE TIES THAT BIND

Cutting the Gordian Knot followed by embracing change are integral endeavors in changing manufacturing performance measurement. It is now useful to address some mechanisms used by managers in leading-edge organizations to help them break Gordian Knots and embrace change. These mechanisms or hints from practice are called *the ties that bind;* they are the strings that management can pull to make things change, regardless of the current set of performance measures.

A characteristic of Gordian Knot cutting cases can be called the *umbrella-holding function.* Someone in the organization holds an umbrella over people below him or her, so these people can adopt new measures and implement new action programs— unfettered by existing measurements that will be unfavorable. One high-level (and therefore large umbrella) example involved a division manager who abolished use of the existing financial budgets inside his division, even though he had to report to corporate headquarters in those very terms. He told his people he did not want them to use those tools again. Instead, they were to develop actions and measures to support lead-time reduction, inventory reduction, faster throughput, higher quality, and better support/identification with customer needs. This manager was convinced that pursuing these goals would lead to better success in the marketplace and improved bottom-line results. That is, he believed these were the leaders or drivers and the financial goals were the followers or passengers. He demonstrated the strength of his belief by discontinuing the calculation of many of the traditional factory measures (such as labor variances).

> Another umbrella-holding example at a lower level was a supervisor who was being criticized by her boss for the varying labor efficiencies in her department. She said nothing about this to the

people working for her, because she knew that the worst reported efficiencies always occurred when the department made a rapid introduction of new products. Here was a case where the workers were doing an excellent job, but the measurement system said otherwise. The supervisor wanted to continue doing an excellent job and so did not expose her workers to measures that were at odds with this belief.

A pilot project is another form of umbrella holding for many companies. Stating that some project is a pilot often implies that standard measures will be held in abeyance for at least some period. Also, often a greater degree of latitude is given to the scope and definition of a pilot. An example is provided by a just-in-time flow line where labor utilization measures deteriorated after the flow line was implemented. However, new measures for quality, throughput time, and inventory were established and significantly improved.

Umbrella holding in many cases results in hiding measures from some part of the organization. That is, the measures are withheld from people at lower management levels, not higher levels, which would have ethical, if not legal, implications. The holder has to believe that the long-term results will be good enough to justify having gone outside of the formal systems and procedures of the company. To some extent, umbrella holding is a risky action—one associated with company rebels. It does, however, appear to be necessary in many cases.

In some enterprises, umbrella holding is almost institutionalized. Perhaps these firms have a canopy in place. One example witnessed in several companies is to place a great deal of attention on "suppliers" and "customers"—in every business activity. Thus, two customers of a subassembly department are the final assembly department and the distribution department that ships replacement subassemblies to customers. Similarly, one of its suppliers is the department that makes the basic metal parts and another is an outside vendor that supplies component parts. The subassembly department is in continuing conversations with both its suppliers and its customers to find ways to make things better. Better implies that the customers will ask for new features and services, and these have to be built into the measures by which the department is to be evaluated.

This linkage of customers and suppliers in the search for continual improvement plays a fundamental role in changing performance measures.

If the linkage indicates improvement runs counter to existing measures, this is considered prima facie evidence that it is time to change the measure. That is, as a canopy, this approach provides institutionalized encouragement to changing performance measures. Such canopies make it less necessary for individuals to hold up umbrellas and take the accompanying risks.

The concept that everyone in the company has at least one customer and is a customer to others provides a horizontal linkage across the organization, based on the value added—as seen through the eyes of the person who receives the value.

This is in contrast to the more usual vertical linkages in organizations based on functional structures (that is, the silos). The ultimate emphasis in the horizontal linkage is on the final customer who uses the product, recognizing his or her set of needs and understanding that the set is never static or fully satisfied. The implication for changing performance measurements is that changes are expected (and should be embraced). They are an integral part of the paradigm. When a customer identifies anything that would enhance the bundle of goods and services provided by the supplier, a new criterion and a shift in what is measured is appropriate.

People do not like change, and in many companies, especially large diversified ones, the performance measurement system may be one of the principal points of stability. Old hands have a vested interest in preserving the status quo. Furthermore, especially in diversified businesses, financial performance measures may be the only common denominator for integration and comparison. In companies with only one line of business, change should be easier. Also, firms that are in more dynamic industries, such as electronics, are more aware of the need to change performance measures than firms in relatively stable industries like heavy chemicals. All this implies that the rate of change in performance measurement is situation-dependent.

Another source of resistance to changes in performance measurement is the need to change the data elements in the measures. This has great significance for computer-based measurement systems. Standard systems can be expected to be out of date and to inhibit progress in many cases. We have seen several examples where managers turned to personal computers in order to get the needed measures. This leads to another feature of environments that support changes. Top managers need to be more willing to give up detail and be less able to aggregate and disaggregate measures throughout the organization. There is usually some act of faith that long-run improvements are the goal, that they will occur, and that they can be measured in gross financial terms such as bottom-line results.

Two complementary approaches seem to support more rapid evolution in performance measurement. The first is top down, where managers cut Gordian Knots and hold large umbrellas and canopies for their workers. The second is bottom up, where typically some very desirable action or new approach to manufacturing is clearly seen as being inhibited by existing measurements. In this case, some manager either hoists a smaller umbrella, believing in the long-run good that will be accomplished, or the organization has canopy mechanisms (customer-supplier) that allow existing measures to be replaced. The top-down approach is required for large, fundamental changes, better supports the discard of obsolete measures, and allows a broader evolution in measures, actions, and strategy. However, it is the bottom-up case that leads to institutionalization of change. Thus, the best hope for changes in the performance measurement system comes from the combination of top-down and bottom-up activity.

Firms need to bring their metrics into alignment with strategies and with the major action programs being undertaken to improve competitive effectiveness. In many cases, performance measurements are impeding the achievement of fundamental corporate objectives.

> Firms are frustrated with cost accounting measures of performance because performance measurement is bigger than accounting.

It is not sufficient for the measurements to be neutral, to not impede. It is essential to formulate performance measures that encourage rapid learning.

Tinkering with the cost accounting system is both inefficient and ineffective in the pursuit of performance measurement for manufacturing excellence.

Manufacturing companies need to get better and to do so faster. This requires that every person in the organization use his or her abilities to a continually higher degree. Everyone needs to work smarter, and increasing the abilities of all employees needs to be seen as an investment that is at least as important as any other. Making this happen requires that management recognize its leadership responsibilities for making the fundamental alterations required in measurement systems.

Management must face up to cutting the Gordian Knot.

It will also be necessary to go beyond the first cut, to where change is the norm. It is imperative that direction for change be provided, that the change process be recognized for its contribution to the well-being of the enterprise, and that mechanisms for speeding the change process be established and nurtured.

Getting better faster means embracing change.

CHAPTER 3

MEASUREMENT AT WANG[1]

Wang Laboratories was experiencing very rough times as this book went to press. Shrinking margins and major debt forced a major restructuring program, including a $237 million cost savings plan based on facility closings and deep personnel cuts. (Figure 3–1 provides an 11-year review of Wang's financial performance.) Although Wang's problems are much more severe than most, it is not alone. A general malaise has affected the computer industry. Similar plans for restructuring are beginning to be seen throughout the world.

This book is mostly about major successes in the performance measurement arena, but it is often illuminating to examine cases where all the pieces did not fit together. Wang did not tumble into catastrophic losses in 1989 without warning. The problems were signalled in both the earnings in 1985 and beyond and in the financial and technology press.

Wang management responded with a slate of actions that included new manufacturing programs. As an integral part in the quest for manufacturing excellence, Wang began experimenting with major changes in the way manufacturing perfor-

---

[1]We are indebted to Kelvin F. Cross, of Judson & Howard, and Richard L. Lynch, of Wang Laboratories, Inc., who developed the SMART system described in this chapter. We are also grateful for the contributions made by Harry Chou and Bob Aspell, also from Wang. Parts of the chapter are based on presentations made by Messrs. Aspell, Chou, and Lynch at the Boston University 75th Anniversary Conference, "Implementing Manufacturing Strategies: Breaking the Performance Measurement Barriers," Tyngsboro, Mass., October 20 and 21, 1988. Other references are "The SMART Way to Define and Sustain Success," by Cross and Lynch, *National Productivity Review,* Winter 1988–89; and "Accounting for Competitive Performance," also by Cross and Lynch, *Journal of Cost Management for the Manufacturing Industry,* Spring 1989.

FIGURE 3–1
Wang's Financial Performance, 1979–1989

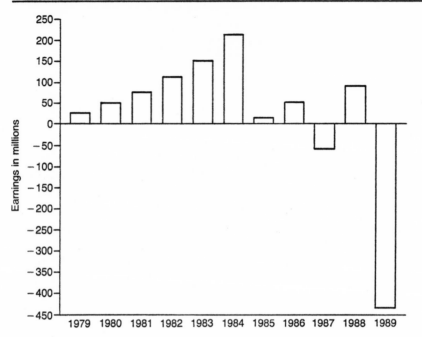

mance was to be measured. The system devised at Wang and the process designed to implement it are well worth studying. The backdrop of Wang's troubles, however, serve as a reminder that a good measurement system is necessary to success in world class competition, but it is not sufficient.

Wang clearly recognized the need for changes in manufacturing methods. However, a fundamental shift in the culture of manufacturing was required, and that need drove a program to change the performance measurement system. Changing performance measures was not the only action Wang took toward manufacturing improvement. The company lowered inventories, tightened expense controls, cut product costs as a percent of revenue, reduced obsolescence costs, and increased research and development outlays.[2]

---

[2]Wang Laboratories, Inc., *1988 Annual Report*.

The final result of executing these programs, and how the competitive situation plays out for Wang, remains to be seen. In any event, there was, and *is,* a need for manufacturing to play a role in making this firm as strong as possible. Wang's approach to devising a new performance measurement system as part of its strategic program reflected its centralized nature. It is not described here as recommended action for all firms in similar circumstances. Rather, the Wang story illustrates the *process* of developing a new kind of performance measurement system. It reflects a conscious effort to coordinate strategies, actions, and measures.

> The primary shift in Wang manufacturing began with an interest in implementing JIT actions in the main factory. This effort led to an understanding that the present system of measurement was inhibiting implementation of these new manufacturing concepts. What was then needed was a change in strategic focus: One that "continually translated the voice of the customer into appropriate operational requirements." This change in strategic focus now supports changes in specific actions—as well as a new measurement system.

The Wang story is divided into three parts. It begins with the *actions*—because that is where the Wang efforts to improve manufacturing began. In this case, the spotlight is on JIT, which Wang calls its "EPIC System." Included are why this change in manufacturing was required, the connections with strategy, how EPIC was implemented, and how all of this supported changes in performance measurement.

The second part of the story focuses on the measurements implemented and the resultant system for performance measurement developed at Wang. The reasons changes were essential, the keys to success in the change, and the ways in which the Wang measurement system nurtures continual learning or improvement are described in this part.

The final part of the story details the lessons illustrated in Wang's experience. In particular, the interactions between strategy, actions, and measures will be bolstered, as will the three-phase change model developed in Chapter 2.

THE EPIC JUST-IN-TIME SYSTEM

EPIC is an acronym created by Wang; it stands for Experimental Process Improvement Challenge. The words are well-chosen, particularly in the case of *experimental*. The EPIC system for implementing just-in-time at Wang was established as an experiment. As an experiment, EPIC was allowed to deviate from the traditions of corporate culture in many regards, including the ways in which equipment purchases were justified and the choices of measurements used to evaluate progress. *Process improvement* was the goal, and the *challenge* was to achieve significant process improvements—without new capital expenditures—that would have a definitive marketplace payoff.

The Competitive Dictates

As a player in the highly competitive worldwide computer industry, Wang faced a new set of competitive challenges in the mid-1980s. It experienced an explosive growth in product mix, shorter product life cycles, new product technology, stronger global competition, increased pressures on product costs, and major decreases in overall profitability.

Responding to these challenges required a manufacturing strategy that was consistent with meeting increased demands for higher quality products, as well as accelerating the development and introduction of new products. It was also necessary to become much more flexible in the ability to respond to the vagaries of the marketplace, to reduce controllable costs, to focus factories, and to improve management of company assets.

Establishing a manufacturing culture and infrastructure that were consistent with this strategy was another kind of challenge: the one reflected in the "C" of EPIC. Management became convinced that manufacturing must adopt a JIT philosophy as well as JIT systems, so faster throughput could be achieved. This would necessitate continuous flow operations, with minimal changeover times. EPIC additionally required processes that would not go down and quality levels that would ensure little lost time because of rework. To support EPIC, Wang needed vendors that would deliver significantly higher quality materials. Wang also needed a build-to-order approach to servicing its customers instead of carrying large buffer inventories. Achieving all of these changes is an ongoing challenge; the need to view this as an experiment should also be apparent.

The EPIC System[3]

The EPIC system is a classic JIT approach, in this case for the manufacture of printed circuit board assemblies. The original program employed seven EPIC lines at Wang's largest facility in Lowell, Massachusetts. Each was dedicated to a family of circuit boards. An EPIC line typically had about 20 employees assigned to it, and the workers were cross-trained so a variety of jobs can be accomplished by the same worker. The number of jobs each worker can do was continually expanded, and worker pay was tied to this broadening of skills. The layout of the lines was U-shaped, supporting communication among the workers.

The original EPIC lines were responsible for all in-circuit test and rework, as opposed to the prior approach at Wang, where specialized areas were set up for these purposes. No circuit boards were started into the assembly process until all component parts were available. Earlier, part kits were issued to the floor with shortages, and boards were sometimes built to a partial state awaiting the receipt of needed parts. All of this stopped with EPIC. Boards were completed within three days of being issued to the floor. Moreover, *all* of them were finished. In the past, the average throughput time for circuit board assembly was about 20 working days, but some boards were in process for considerably longer. The average reduction in flow time and work-in-process inventory under EPIC was 85 percent.

The Implementation Process and the New Culture

The results achieved in EPIC are impressive, but are not particularly unusual for JIT success stories. Of more interest here is the role of measurement—and how the *changing* of measure-

---

[3]For further information on EPIC, see Kelvin F. Cross, "Wang Scores EPIC Success with Circuit Board Assembly Redesign," *Industrial Engineering,* January 1988.

ments was imperative for EPIC implementation to become a reality.

There was widespread agreement that the existing system of measures was inhibiting the adoption of newer concepts in manufacturing such as JIT.

A survey of the manufacturing managers at Wang indicated 90 percent believed the measurement systems were inadequate for implementing and supporting strategic operations such as the EPIC system.

The company needed to define measures in terms relevant to the day-to-day decisions made on the factory floor.

The mismatch between highly responsive manufacturing operations—those that provided timely responses to customer requests with minimal inventories—and existing measures that favored high utilization of people and equipment created an impasse that could be reconciled only by a change in performance measurements.

Wang went into the EPIC implementation process with a belief that both top-down and bottom-up establishment of measures was the best way to achieve long-run objectives.

This implies a fundamental change in attitude. Measures will differ across organizational units, and they will continually evolve. Thus, power is shared, and every measure must be regarded as a provisional or probationary one.

The entire culture in manufacturing had to change.

JIT represented a fundamental shift in what was regarded as vital; customer satisfaction and velocity of material were most important, not utilization of equipment or personnel. Achieving these dictates at Wang involved acknowledgment of the constraints inherent in its forms of organization.

Vertical organizational structures inhibited activities that were integrative or horizontal in nature, such as the flows of materials and new product introductions.

Wang embraced the customer-supplier linkage approach described in Chapter 2 as a technique for better understanding horizontal connections based on work flow. This had implications for both the EPIC system design and the appropriate performance metrics.

The entire notion of traditional product cost as a measure of operational performance had to be unlearned.

The cost focus had to shift to one based on waste, the costs that can be avoided. These are now the basis for evaluating cost performance in manufacturing, not costs over which the factory has no control.

In order for the EPIC implementation to occur, top management at Wang needed to be committed to the effort, to encourage experimentation, to set aside the traditional measures of manufacturing effectiveness and the measures for particular managers, to encourage personal commitment by the lower level managers, and to find ways to establish external evaluations of progress. This last feature was supported through use of a management consultant who had knowledge of other companies that had adopted JIT approaches in manufacturing.

As the EPIC system was developed and implemented, the mismatch with measures became increasingly apparent.

The standard cost accounting system was clearly out of touch with the manufacturing strategy.

It was based on financial information that was not relevant to improved quality, better customer support, or faster throughput. The data were too aggregated, and they came in too late for any real corrective actions. Many crucial pieces of information were not collected, and the data were organized around functional or vertical organizational structures. They were not in a form that supported problem solving focused on horizontal goals such as how to reduce final assembly failure rates attributable to purchased parts.

The most fundamental flaw with the existing measurement system was its inability to guide the company in implementing the EPIC process.

Progress could not be adequately measured with the existing system. Moreover, the archaic measures often indicated things were awry, when they were proceeding quite well. For example, some quality costs increased, such as those that improved the incoming quality of components. One simply can not look at such costs in isolation; the impact on downstream manufacturing has to be included. Such measurement system flaws can be overcome in the short run by simply ignoring the measures in the interest of experimentation. In the longer run, however, it is necessary to make fundamental changes in the metrics and in the approach to continually modifying them.

THE WANG MEASUREMENT SYSTEM

The success of the EPIC JIT lines at Wang led to an unobstructed perception of the existing measurement system's faults. Wang started with an interest in actions, consistent with a strategy, and the results led to an obvious need to change measurements. The company attacked this problem by developing a new measurement approch it calls the Strategic Measurement Analysis & Reporting Technique (SMART).

The SMART Hierarchy

The objectives of SMART are to integrate both financial and nonfinancial reporting, to link manufacturing to the strategic goals for the company, to concentrate the measurement system design on satisfying customer needs, and to develop a system that fosters constant evolution—both in terms of what is important and how the enterprise is to be measured. SMART is designed with a hierarchy of objectives and measures.

Figure 3–2 depicts the Wang hierarchy in the form of a pyramid. At the top of the pyramid is the corporate vision, which defines what markets the company will compete in, product scope, and services provided. The vision in turn leads to goals for the marketplace and detailed financial goals. These goals are strategic business objectives. They lead to the business operating system objectives of customer satisfaction, flexibility, and productivity. Implied in the term *business operating system ob-*

FIGURE 3–2
The SMART Hierarchy

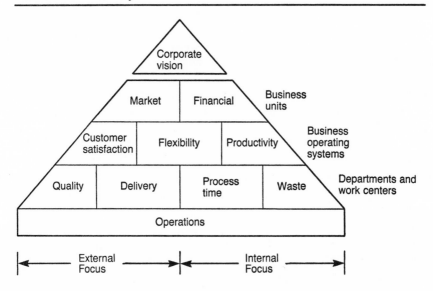

jectives is a need to work across functional boundaries, with a horizontal focus on work flows, to achieve goals. The last level in the hierarchy is departmental and work center criteria. These include quality, delivery, process time, and waste. The only category in which cost is considered is the last one.

For each of these goals, objectives, or criteria, Wang needs one or more measures. Moreover, Wang recognizes that each measure will be imperfect; over time, all measures will be improved to better serve the future requirements of its customers.

Detailed Measures

Quality at Wang encompasses more than conformance to specifications.

> The overriding maxim is to "translate the voice of the customer into appropriate company requirements."

Examples of measures used to meet this objective are the percent "plug and play" achieved in final assembly, the parts per thousand (or other denominator) accepted in purchased parts, and the percentage of targets met in research and development. These examples illustrate the emphasis given to quality in *all* areas of the company, not just manufacturing.

Similarly, delivery is seen as a goal to which all organizational units need to aspire in their own ways.

> Delivery at Wang translates to quantity and timeliness, in particular to the extent to which correct amounts are delivered on time.

Examples include the percentage of end products delivered in a particular time frame as compared to the master production schedule, the percentage of all component parts delivered to an assembly line at the appropriate time, the percentage of engineering change orders completed on time, and the percentage of customer orders "delivered" through credit checking as compared to the standard time for this activity.

> Process time is concerned with the time required to complete work from the time it is requested.

The focus on request means the time meter can start before typical organizational units have total responsibility. For example, although a manufacturing subassembly department would be held accountable only for the time after receipt of necessary materials until the order is closed, at the business operating system level, the focus would be on the *overall* time; that is, the purchasing lead time, plus the planning lead time, plus stock preparation, plus assembly, and so on. The Wang approach, however, focuses attention on the overall problem; that is, on the *horizontal work flow*. The throughput time for production from request for an item, the setup time in a work cell, the time to design a new product, the time to bring a new market concept to the marketplace, or the time to process an invoice are all examples of these measures.

For the purposes of performance measurement, cost at Wang is not focused on the traditional accounting costs for products, with all of the attendant problems of allocation.

The cost emphasis is on any extra or excess costs incurred in order to satisfy the required quality and delivery requirements of the customers.

These costs are considered to be waste. The underlying reason for the distinction is that costs are necessary, but waste is not. The best that any person or organizational unit can do is to minimize the waste it generates. Examples include yield losses in manufacturing, rejected materials in purchasing, inventory costs (under the belief in zero inventories), and the total costs associated with engineering changes (because the design should have been right in the first place).

Pilot Results

Implementation of the SMART system for performance measurement resulted in several changes at Wang.

Approximately 40 percent of the existing measures were discarded, including purchased price variance, labor productivity, and virtually all of the standard cost accounting variances for operating feedback.

Of those that remained, many were redefined, particularly those relating to quality and cost. Additionally, new measures were added, to focus attention of the horizontal variety. That is, the problems were associated with work flows that cross functional lines, such as the process of new product introduction.

Examples of new metrics are new measures of inventory turns, plug and play rates, material availability, waste rates, and process times.

One of the benefits achieved was better communication across organizational units that historically had not seen the need for close coordination, such as between design engineering and manufacturing. The priorities were also sharpened as a result of the better communication (and because of the dictates of a JIT system where problems are no longer hidden). The overriding spotlight on the customer (and *future* customer needs) also had benefits. This proactive focus enabled people to better understand the need for certain actions, such as better response time, the impact of reducing lead times and inventory levels, and the need for working together to achieve these ends.

> SMART crystallized the needs for new information collection, the gaps in management information systems (MIS), and the places where these MIS were collecting obsolete information.

For example, when material flows through the shop in 3 days instead of 20, the needs for material tracking and shop floor priority systems become virtually nonexistent. Many information-gathering and analysis functions formerly done by staff groups became a part of the basic manufacturing infrastructure. For example, much of the quality control that had been accomplished by staff personnel now became integrated into the EPIC lines.

SMART did not attempt to change the financial reporting associated with standard fiduciary accounting. However, the *basis* for generating these reports did change.

> Instead of creating financial reports from detailed material movements through the factory, a much more simplified approach was taken.

Because little inventory exists on the manufacturing floor or in the warehouses, the accounting for financial purposes is greatly facilitated. SMART is independent of the systems used for external reporting and will always remain so because SMART is seen as a continually changing system, one that must not be constrained by tradition. Instead, the measurement system needs to foster learning and couple measures to the particular actions and strategies of the time.

Since the focus for improvement in SMART is horizontal, as opposed to vertical (consolidated supplier-customer networks instead of functional groupings), the underlying logic for some traditional organizational forms starts to fade. Separation of quality organizations from scheduling and manufacturing is one example of an eroding distinction. Another is the way in which MIS personnel and resources are deployed in the pursuit of continuing excellence. Finally, linkages with vendors in the interest of vendor partnerships cross even company borders. In all of this, performance measurement is critical. It is critical to have the right systems, with the right overall nucleus and measures. The SMART view of the customer is consistent with these dictates.

LESSONS

In this final section, the Wang example is used to reinforce the ideas and three-phase framework for changing performance measures that were developed in Chapters 1 and 2. The intent is to bolster the understanding of those concepts, so subsequent chapters can build on this understanding.

Strategies, Actions, and Measures

The Wang example is primarily one where the actions, namely the introduction of just-in-time manufacturing methods, provided the driving force for changing performance measurements. On closer examination, however, one also sees the impact of the manufacturing strategy. Wang clearly perceived the need to overhaul manufacturing to meet the challenges of the global marketplace.

The company faced increasing hostility in its competitive environment, including a significant reduction in product life cycle time, technology that more quickly became outdated, severe cost pressure from reduced margins, and a need to help customers solve their problems—as opposed to simply providing a fairly standardized product. All of these had profound implications for manufacturing.

> New levels of quality, reduced overhead costs, expedited new product introductions, and greater flexibility were part of the mandate.

The pursuit of these goals required formulation of an action agenda. This, in turn, led directly to the need for changing performance measures.

At the beginning of Wang's efforts, there was a significant lack of congruence between the strategy, actions, and measures.

The measures point of the triangle was most out of step. The actions supported development of a more competitively focused strategy, but the accounting-based measurement system did not. The survey of manufacturing managers demonstrated general disapproval of the existing measures.

An interesting issue is the chicken-and-egg question regarding changes in measures versus changes in actions and or strategy. That is, which precedes which? At Wang, the focus on actions and strategy stimulated the need for measurement change. This is consistent with the experiences of other firms. Changing measurements as an abstract exercise does not have many champions. It seems to be a much hotter topic when it is perceived as the obstacle to progress, or as a lever for implementing a new strategy.

Once the measurement change problem is seen positively, it acts as an accelerator for learning. Wang started with the view that present performance measures were impeding progress, but the restriction was in terms of achieving a well-defined set of actions. The second order understanding is that there is no ultimate weapon, and that new actions (and strategic objectives) will be continuously delineated.

> The goal of a measurement system is not only to conform to evolving actions and strategies, but also to nurture this learning.

The measurement system should help the firm adapt to the competitive environment—faster.

Lessons from the Manufacturing Futures Survey

The second major section in Chapter 1 dealt with important conclusions about worldwide manufacturing derived from the Boston University Manufacturing Futures Project. These themes are also well-illustrated in the Wang example.

The North American survey data indicate improvements in quality, manufacturing strategy, and new product development have received much greater emphasis over the past five years. Also indicated in the survey data are increased adoption of time-based competition, the provision of better customer service and an enhanced bundle of goods and services, and a growing need to work across organizational boundaries.

All of these trends were manifested at Wang.

> Quality and flexibility were the main drivers that led to the EPIC project.

The need to formulate a consistent manufacturing strategy to drive the EPIC action program was also well-understood. The customer focus was expressly directed to enhancing the bundle of goods and services provided to the customers and to involving those clients in defining the best bundle. The switch to a make-to-order form of manufacturing allowed each customer order to become increasingly customized—to reflect his or her unique bundle.

> Working across organizational boundaries was vitally important at Wang.

The company placed great emphasis on the concept of horizontal linkages (supplier-customer networks) instead of the vertical linkages associated with usual organizational forms. Included were the horizontal focus on work streams, such as the flow of materials; the interactions between circuit board fabrication, testing, and rework; and the introduction of new products in a JIT manufacturing environment.

Work Force Organization

Work force organization issues relate to deploying overhead personnel, improving the use of knowledge workers, increasing the knowledge work done by all employees, and developing the "whole person concept," where people are paid for their brains as well as their backs and where the goal is to constantly increase the amount of staff work incorporated into the basic infrastructure of manufacturing. More and more firms are attempting to reduce the number of staff personnel assigned to both quality and manufacturing planning and control. Chapter 2 also proposed a goal of continual learning or improvement and a performance measure for JIT lines based on maximizing the idle time of all people on the line. The intent of this measure is to create capacity for the workers to take on more staff work, such as quality control and scheduling, and to invest in worker training. The overall goal is to learn faster.

Many of these ideas were found at Wang.

> The EPIC JIT lines resulted in an overall reduction in the number of people required to make the products. They also allowed a reduction in staff work to support the circuit board lines.

Staff workers were less frequently found tucked away in offices, and more likely found on the shop floor, influencing the action. Each EPIC line had a manufacturing engineer assigned to it; it was his or her job to work on continual improvement and to solve problems *immediately.*

Quality became a basic part of the job, and so did any necessary rework. Raw materials were issued to one end of the line and fully tested circuit boards came off the other end, with any necessary rework having been routinely executed. No extra routings or departments were required, and paperwork was kept to a minimum. Feedback from quality and rework tasks was immediate, so mistakes would not be repeated unnecessarily.

Explicit adoption of the idle time maximization measure did not take place, but many of its results were achieved. There was an increased emphasis on training, as well as a pay for skills approach that strongly encouraged cross training. An EPIC team was just that, an independent *team,* with primary allegiance to the group and with a learning-based goal of constant improvement.

> There was a clear understanding that the job of the line was not just constant output.

When steady state was achieved, the expectation was to take on something new—a new product, a new process, or a new task presently done for the team by an outside service organization—in addition to turning out top-quality products on schedule.

A further example of a fundamental change in work force organization is seen in the different attitudes toward tools such as management by objectives (MBO) after implementation of EPIC and SMART. MBO has a vertical orientation. A manager and his or her subordinates determine, on a joint basis, a set of goals by which the subordinates' performance will be evaluated. The determination is based on how achievements by the subordinate will enhance or support the objectives of the manager. The MBO approach is sometimes criticized because coordination among the managers and subordinates can be difficult, occasionally leading to obvious conflicts of interest. At Wang, the implementation of EPIC and SMART highlighted these conflicts with a new potency.

> The focus on horizontal linkages and work flows means the joint determination of actions can no longer be made in an organizational "silo" hierarchy.

There is a top-down orientation in that the overall business objectives are set at the top of the organization, but the direction for attaining these goals is not functional. The orientation is on business performance as a whole, rather than on any individual or group of individuals, and the guiding beacon for improvement is customer satisfaction—and continual improvement in customer satisfaction.

SMART is not intended to provide assessment of individuals. In the closely coupled EPIC system, it is the overall effort that is important. Attempts at isolating precisely who is most responsible for achieving improvements are left to the subjective opinions of the EPIC managers.

> The measurement emphasis in EPIC is on group performance, and some of the group members are not formally a part of the EPIC team (for example, design engineers or materials managers).

SMART eschews departmental objective setting. This approach, typically supported by cost accounting-based systems, too often leads to a long list of negative performance variances that are too aggregated, come too late, and are too often determined by factors over which the department has little or no control.

> The emphasis in SMART is on constant improvement, where the measure of precisely what to improve is changing.

It is not based on some static definition that can be readily compared to historical data. The presumption is that if things are done right, next year will be so different that it makes little sense to compare it to a string of past years.

The Three-Phase Change Model

In the change model presented in Chapter 2, the phases through which firms seem to pass are first a prephase one, where complaining or grousing about the current measurements occurs. There are indications that this phase took place at Wang. The most notable illustration was in the survey of Wang manufacturing managers where 90 percent believed the present system of performance measures was impeding progress toward where they individually believed the company needed to go.

Phase one, tinkering, was also a stage through which Wang passed. It took time for the concept of cost to shake off linkages to traditional accounting definitions, and this process was by no means complete throughout the Wang organization. The transition in such a situation will be complete only when the lines are no longer viewed as experimental. Results should prove the wisdom of the experiment and lead to migration of the concepts throughout the organization.

There are many illustrations of Gordian Knot cutting at Wang.

> The pyramid in SMART is clearly based on nonfinancial as well as financial measures.

The hierarchy has departmental and work center performance based on nonfinancial metrics. Quality, delivery, and process time are distinctly nonfinancial. Cost as used at this level is also nonfinancial, if the definition of financial is that the data will feed external financial reporting. The emphasis is on waste; that is, the cost that can be avoided. The business operating systems are also largely nonfinancial in orientation. Customer satisfaction and flexibility are obviously nonfinancial. Productivity could be either financial or nonfinancial depending upon the ways in which the measures are calculated. At Wang, the productivity measures definitively include the management of time, which is not a financial concept.

> Wang has recognized the clear need for two systems, based on two needs: nonfinancial for internal effectiveness and learning, and financial for outside reporting.

The need for two separate measurement systems is further supported by the business unit and corporate vision levels at the top of the pyramid. Here, the financial goals and measures are only half of the corporate vision. The marketplace is the other half. This half will by necessity be assessed through nonfinancial measures.

Phase three, embracing change, can also be seen at Wang. Some elimination of measures (20 percent) was achieved, while new metrics were added and refined. Continual focus on the customers is another example.

> At Wang, a proactive approach was taken toward eliminating measures.

The customer's needs are to be anticipated, Wang is to satisfy them before they are demanded, and the measures need to encourage evolution in the bundle of goods and services provided. This means new measures will be needed and old ones must be discarded.

Wang also illustrates top-down and bottom-up design and implementation of new measures. The company placed a strong emphasis on ownership of the measurement process by the operating managers. Wang managers believed that measures are equally important to actions in the achievement of long-term improvements.

> Overall goals are set from the top, but the day-to-day objectives and measures are the responsibility of the people on the floor.

These measures will never be perfect. Managers should strive toward excellence within an existing set of measures, and they should strive to constantly improve the metrics. Managers, working together, can best define the measures that drive their actions.

The Ties that Bind

The last section of Chapter 2 dealt with methods observed for institutionalizing change in performance measurement systems. Several companies have used experiments or pilots as one means to break out of the constraints imposed by traditional performance metrics. Wang falls into this group.

The EPIC system was billed as an experiment from day one.

This allowed the managers of these lines to work toward whatever was seen as necessary for attainment of the market-place goals. It was not necessary to justify capital expenditures in the same way, to account for every minute of direct labor, to explain accounting variances, or to beat up vendors to attain better prices.

Wang also illustrated the use of a canopy described in Chapter 2.

The linking of everyone in the organization as customers and suppliers puts emphasis on horizontal flows and their improvement.

When improvement is impeded by a particular measure, this indicates the problem may be the measure; it may be time to change metrics. A domino effect is sought, where actions drive measurement changes, which in turn drive actions. All of this is, in turn, piloted by an overriding strategy. But strategy is also not a static concept. It can and should evolve. Part of the evolution will be driven by external forces, but another part can be determined internally, as manufacturing becomes increasingly a competitive weapon.

In closing this chapter on Wang, it is useful to return to the company's financial crisis. As this book goes to press, family control at Wang has been diminished and the firm is earnestly engaged in turnaround management. Many people are losing their jobs and the change to the corporate culture is enormous.

Whether Wang can survive in a recognizable form remains to be seen. But what will become of the EPIC lines, the drive toward manufacturing improvement, and the SMART system? It is likely that progress on these projects will be suspended. Given the newer competitive dictates, the projects may be sacrificed to actions and measures chosen to meet survival-based cash flow objectives.

The fundamental issue is still to improve manufacturing to meet the demands of world class competition. Some firms will achieve this goal while others will not. Success requires all the pieces to be in place. The strategies have to be good, the actions have to match the strategies, and the measures have to reflect the strategies in the terms of the actions. There are lessons to be learned from Wang's experience, both in its successes and in its trials.

CHAPTER 4

THE PERFORMANCE MEASUREMENT QUESTIONNAIRE: A DIAGNOSTIC TOOL FOR CUTTING THE GORDIAN KNOT

- Seeing the *need* to change performance measures is not enough—a *means* or a *process* for accomplishing the required changes is also necessary.
- The process has to involve the managers who can best evaluate the changes—those who will implement the new measures and be held accountable for them.
- The direction and degree of the change must be agreed upon—the direction needs to be consistent with the strategy and the degree needs to be realistic in terms of what actions can be accomplished.
- The process has to foster consensus building and continual evolution—each situation will be somewhat unique with its own set of opportunities and challenges.

This chapter introduces a *process* for changing performance measurements, the Performance Measurement Questionnaire (PMQ). It works! It has been used in many manufacturing situations, and its process also has been applied recently in marketing, logistics, service, and other contexts.[1]

---

[1] Appendix A provides a complete copy of the Performance Measurement Questionnaire in the form that has been most widely used. Appendix B provides a copy of the questionnaire as it was modified for use in a marketing organization.

The objectives for PMQ can be stated quite simply: to provide a means by which an organization can articulate its improvement needs, determine the extent to which its existing set of measurements is supportive of the necessary improvements, and establish an agenda for improving the measures so they better support achievement of the improvements.

DESIGN OF THE PERFORMANCE MEASUREMENT QUESTIONNAIRE

The PMQ is composed of four major parts. The first part consists of requests for some general data to be used to classify the respondents. These items include the company and location, the hierarchical level of management occupied by the respondent, and the functional area in which the respondent works.

The data on management level and functional affiliation are used to examine the degree of consensus among managerial levels and functional areas.

The rest of the PMQ is based on individual perceptions of what actions are important to improving the competitive effectiveness of the company and the extent to which the measurement systems in the company support or impede achievement of these actions.

Improvement Areas

Part II of the PMQ focuses on competitive priorities and the performance measurement system. In the most widely used version of the PMQ, this section is comprised of 24 items labeled as "improvement areas." They are presented in a center column as in Figure 4–1. On each side of this column, a column of scales made up of the numbers 1 through 7 appears. The column of scales on the left is labeled "long-run importance of improvement." The column of scales on the right is labeled "effect of current performance measures on improvement."

For each of the 24 items, the respondents are asked to circle a number on each scale. On the left-hand scale, respondents are

FIGURE 4–1
Section of Part II of the Performance Measurement Questionnaire

Improvement Areas		
Long-Run Importance of Improvement		Effect of Current Performance Measures on Improvement
None >>> Great		Inhibit >> Support
1 2 3 4 5 6 7	Quality	1 2 3 4 5 6 7
1 2 3 4 5 6 7	Labor efficiency	1 2 3 4 5 6 7
1 2 3 4 5 6 7	Machine efficiency	1 2 3 4 5 6 7

asked to indicate their opinions of the relative degree of importance that improvement in that area (that is, a change in its characteristics) has for the long-term health of the company. The number 1 indicates improvement is unimportant or unnecessary, while the number 7 indicates it is critical to improve in that area.

> For example, if a respondent believed the present levels of quality being achieved in the firm are adequate to meet future competitive requirements, he or she would score this improvement area with a low value, regardless of perceptions of the firm's *absolute* level of quality. If on the other hand, he or she felt that a major improvement was required in this area, it would receive a high score.

On the right-hand scale, the respondents are asked to circle the number that corresponds to the extent to which they believe the plant's current performance measures, taken as a whole, support or inhibit improvement in that area, with 1 indicating inhibition and 7 indicating full support.

Performance Factors

Part III of the PMQ is constructed similarly, but now the reference is to performance factors. These might also be called performance measures, except that the list is comprised of generic measures, some of which the company may not be using, at least under that name. In the most widely used version of the PMQ, a list of 39 potential measures runs down the center of the page.

> The left-hand scale measures the extent to which the respondents believe that achieving excellence in this factor or measure is important for the long-run health of the company, from none (1) to great (7). The right-hand scale measures the extent to which they believe the company emphasizes that measure from none (1) to great (7).

Figure 4–2 provides the first portion of this list of performance factors.

Each improvement area has at least two, if not more, analogous items on the list of performance factors. For example, the improvement area "quality" has "vendor quality," "yields," "conformance to specifications," and "cost of quality" as counterparts in the performance factors section. This redundancy provides better support for analysis of the data.

Personal Performance Metrics

Part IV is labeled "your performance measures." Respondents are asked to record their perceptions of the most important measures against which their individual performance is judged in each of five time frames: daily, weekly, monthly, quarterly, and annually.

FIGURE 4–2
Section of Part III of the Performance Measurement Questionnaire

	Performance Factors	
Relative Importance to the Company		*Emphasis of Measurement*
Very Unimportant Very Important		No Emphasis Major Emphasis
1 2 3 4 5 6 7	Inventory turnover	1 2 3 4 5 6 7
1 2 3 4 5 6 7	Conformance to specifications	1 2 3 4 5 6 7
1 2 3 4 5 6 7	Cost of quality	1 2 3 4 5 6 7

These data are used to reveal the extent to which individuals believe they are evaluated in the same measures that are given in the questionnaire. Another insight gained from Part IV is the degree to which financial as opposed to non-financial measures are used, and for which organizational levels and functions this is true.

Part IV also asks the respondents to make any general comments they have about the questionnaire, performance measurement, or the need for change. This open-ended section provides an appreciation for the degree of cohesiveness around the issues associated with changing performance measurements in the company. It also has, on occasion, provided an avenue for respondents to express their frustrations in ways that are not otherwise available.

ADMINISTRATION OF THE PMQ

The questionnaire is designed so it can be completed in less than half an hour. Typically, it has been administered to groups of respondents, so any questions about the PMQ could be answered. The PMQ has also been administered by mail, but experience supports group administration as the best way to quickly and uniformly gather the data.

The half-hour time frame allows for data to be gathered from a reasonably large percentage of the managerial population in the company. To the extent that participation includes all managers, belief in the results is enhanced. Moreover, the involvement of all managers communicates a significant commitment to change.

The design of the questionnaire incorporates a juxtaposition of "should be" and "is." This focuses attention on a critical review of the deficiencies of the present measurement system. More importantly, it also creates a demand for correction of the measurement problems. If review of the existing measurement system does not lead to improvements, the result is worse than doing nothing, since the frustration level will have been raised significantly.

Administration by outsiders or anonymous response has advantages. The respondents are encouraged to be as frank as possible. The brief, open-ended question in the last section of the questionnaire permits people to express concerns or simply to blow off steam.

The specific items included in Parts II and III are not sacred. In practice, most companies want to tailor these sections to reflect their own priorities and language. In nonmanufacturing applications, the PMQ has been completely altered, not only in the specific items, but also in the number of items and in their descriptions, as seen in the marketing version in Appendix B.

ANALYSIS OF THE PMQ DATA

The PMQ yields a great deal of data, for which a variety of analyses can be conducted, so it is important to remember the primary objectives—articulate improvement needs, determine the extent of support by existing measures, and formulate an agenda for improved measures.

> The PMQ was not designed as a vehicle to collect data for academically rigorous analysis, nor was it intended to lead to the creation of the most sophisticated measurement systems possible.

The PMQ was designed to invoke a process. The analytical results from the PMQ should provide a focus for group discussion that leads to the largest net gain possible for the organization at that time. The PMQ will not, indeed cannot, lead to a new optimal measurement system. Optimality in performance measurement is going to be defined by the company's needs at a particular time.

The analytical tools and procedures are simple, as a conscious matter of design. Averages, ranks, and measures of variation comprise the set of tools. While more sophisticated statistical analyses may be performed, their ability to stimulate managerial interest is limited. Simple statistics are used to conduct four basic types of analysis, which are called alignment, congruence, consensus, and confusion.

Alignment Analysis

The term *alignment* refers to the extent to which a company's strategy, actions, and measures line up with each other (match and are mutually supportive).

> The competitive potency of a strategy is realized only when actions and measures complement the strategy. The goal of alignment analysis is to test the extent of this alignment.

The first step in alignment analysis is to investigate in general terms how well a company's actions and measures complement its strategy. This can be illustrated with the data analysis from one company site. Recall that Part II of the questionnaire requires managers to rate 24 improvement areas in terms of (1) the long-run strategic importance of improvement in that area and (2) the level of support for such improvement provided by the current performance measurement system. After averaging all of the responses, the left-side responses can be rank ordered. The top and bottom 25 percent (quartile) of that rank order list from one company site appear in Figure 4–3.

By using only the top and bottom quartiles, the number of potential issues to examine is reduced by half. Nonetheless, a significant amount of information remains. For example, in Figure 4–3, the plant in question was actively implementing JIT. Flow lines accounted for most of the manufacturing process.

FIGURE 4–3
Congruence with Strategies at One Company Site

Strategic Action Areas Importance of Improvement	
Top Quartile	*Bottom Quartile*
New product introduction	Job responsibilities
Customer satisfaction	Machine efficiency
Product technology	Direct cost reduction
Quality	Environmental control
Integration with customers	labor efficiency
Manufacturing throughput times	Offshore manufacturing

Both management and the work force had received extensive training and education in JIT, TQC, and associated techniques. However, the old performance measurement system remained in place.

The data contained in Figure 4–3 verified that the plant management had correctly absorbed the new strategic imperatives. This demonstrated that there was no mismatch between corporate manufacturing strategy and that perceived at the plant level.

A similar analysis to check for alignment between the strategy and measures uses the data from Part III of the PMQ. However, now it is the top and bottom quartiles of the right-side (emphasis on the measure) response ranks that show how well the current measurement system matches with the strategy (there are 10 performance factors in each quartile).

As shown in Figure 4–4, the emphasis placed on measures in this plant did not align as well with the corporate strategy as did the improvement areas. Some measures, such as "dollars shipped per period," appear in the top quartile when they probably should not, and others, such as "new product introduction,"

FIGURE 4–4
Alignment with Strategies at One Company Site

Performance Factors
Company Emphasis on Measure

Top Quartile	Bottom Quartile
On-time delivery	Direct labor productivity
Safety	Minimize environmental waste
Dollars shipped per period	Vendor lead times
Meet production schedule	Change/setup times
Margins	Indirect labor productivity
Inventory turnover	Number of suppliers
Cost reduction: dollar savings	Environmental monitoring
Return on investment	Sales forecast accuracy
Conformance to specifications	Number of engineering changes
Yields	Number of material part numbers

are not included in the top quartile when they probably should be. Similarly, measures like "vendor lead times" are in the bottom quartile, while "unit labor cost" and "variances" do not appear there.

> These results suggest there is room for improvement in the set of measures used at this company.

The specific improvements are better identified in the Congruence Analysis, which is described next.

Congruence Analysis

The alignment analysis provides a general overview of the consistency between the strategy, actions, and measures. It gives a pulse reading. Specific treatments, however, are suggested by congruence analysis.

> The goal of congruence analysis is to provide a detailed look at how well the measurement system supports an organization's actions and strategy. This is done by examining the difference between the left-side response and the right-side response for each item in Parts II and III of the PMQ.

Significant differences identified in the congruence analysis are called *gaps* or *false alarms*, depending on the nature of the difference. A gap in an improvement area is defined as occurring when the average rated importance of improvement for all respondents significantly exceeds the perceived extent to which the measurement system supports improvement in that area. That is, the left-side score is greater than the right-side score, resulting in a positive difference.

> An improvement area gap signals the need for increased support for improvement in that area from the measurement system.

The opposite condition occurs when the relationship is reversed: measurement system support for improvement exceeds the importance of improvement. This outcome is called a false alarm.

> In a false alarm, the performance measurement system is "ringing," but no real problem exists! The problem is that the performance measurement system is ringing for the wrong reason!

FIGURE 4–5
Gap in Measurement System

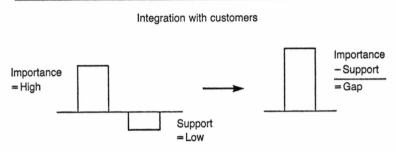

Gaps and false alarms are similarly calculated for the performance factor items in Part III of the questionnaire.

Graphically, gaps and false alarms can be represented in bar charts. In Figure 4–5, the first bar represents the importance of improvement in "integration with customers" compared with the average need for improvement across all 24 improvement areas. The bar rises in a positive direction from a base line indicating that improving the organization's ability to integrate its activities with its customers is more important than the average need for improvement. The second bar descends in the negative direction from its baseline, showing that the measurement system lends less support to improving integration with customers than it does on average for all 24 improvement areas.

> The third bar, which represents the difference between the importance of improvement and the support provided by the measurement system for customer integration, rises significantly above its baseline. There is a significant gap.

Figure 4–3 showed the importance of improvement in this area; we now see it is not well-supported by existing measurement systems.

Figure 4–6 illustrates a false alarm for a performance factor, "direct labor productivity," identified by analysis of data from Part III of the PMQ using the same graphical approach.

> The emphasis placed on direct labor productivity by the measurement system exceeds the importance of excellence in that measure for the long-term health of the organization.

FIGURE 4–6
False Alarm in Measurement System

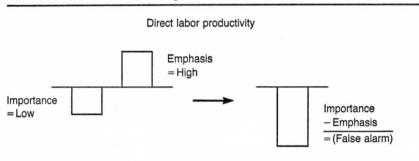

FIGURE 4–7
Control Limits for Gaps and False Alarms

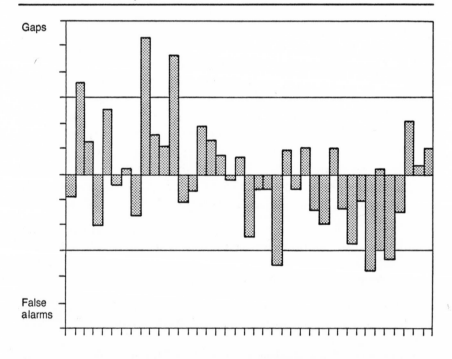

The third bar, which reflects the difference between the importance of an improvement area or performance factor and the degree to which the measurement system supports it, is the focus of attention in Figure 4–7. The average difference for all 39 items in Part III is represented by the baseline.

A bar rising above the line indicates a gap, a difference for that item greater than the average of all differences. Conversely, a bar extending below the baseline, indicating a false alarm, shows an average difference for that item in the lower half of the list.

Figure 4–7 also shows two control limits drawn in to isolate the most significant gaps and false alarms. The location of these control limits is somewhat arbitrary; the limits have been selected so the focus is placed on only a few gaps and false alarms. As an organization improves the fit of its measurement system to its strategy and actions and the differences decrease, these lines might be drawn closer to the baseline, to encourage continued improvement.

Figure 4–8 lists gaps and false alarms for the same plant depicted in Figure 4–3. The list differs from the strategy alignment list in Figure 4–3.

The gaps and false alarms analysis, in a sense, ignores the places where the current system is already doing an adequate job—in this plant, for example, in measuring customer satisfaction—and focuses attention on areas where improvement is possible.

> The list of gaps and false alarms implicitly prioritizes areas where new measures need to be created and areas where existing measures are candidates for being discarded.

FIGURE 4–8
Gaps and False Alarms in Strategic Action Areas at One Company Site

Strategic Action Areas Importance of Improvement Minus Support for Improvement	
Gaps *Top Quartile*	*False Alarms* *Bottom Quartile*
New product introduction	Inventory management
Product technology	Machine efficiency
Overhead cost reduction	Labor efficiency
Integration with suppliers	Environmental control
Performance measurement	Offshore manufacturing
Information systems	Direct cost reduction

If that list is too long, it can be reduced further to, say, the top three and the bottom three. An alternative, the control chart illustrated in Figure 4–7, has already been described.

Consensus Analysis

The next cut in the analysis of the PMQ involves grouping the data by management level or by functional area.

> The goal of consensus analysis is to contrast the perceptions between hierarchical levels and across functional organizations.

Comparison of results across levels or functions can expose points where poor communication of strategies and actions has resulted in a systematic lack of consensus. However, not all differences across levels or functions signal a serious communication problem. Legitimate differences between groups have been observed that directly result from the conversion of strategy to action across levels or functions. Such appropriate differences are called *strategy/tactic relationships*. It is also possible to observe differences that are caused by poor communication, but that are artifacts of local glitches in the communication process rather than the results of systematic defects in that process. Such differences are called *phantom inconsistencies*.

Figure 4–9 provides an example of a systematic lack of consensus across management levels.

> The plant's top management identified the importance of the performance factor "indirect labor productivity" as great, while lower levels of management in the plant were far less concerned about this measure.

During a followup discussion at this factory, the difference turned out to result from a general lack of awareness about the importance of indirect labor productivity. This effect was made worse by association with the "correct" perception of the reduced importance of direct labor productivity. In this case, the failure in communication occurred in the top-down dissemination process. However, there are also instances where the communications fault has been a bottom-up break where upper manage-

FIGURE 4–9
Consensus across Management Levels (Indirect Labor Productivity)

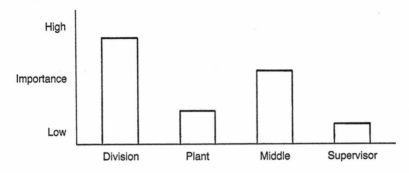

ment had not fully understood the relationships between measures and the actions required by the strategy.

Another way a systematic lack of consensus between levels of management hierarchy can be identified is to find those instances where the rank data consistently increase or decrease with management level. That is, it is helpful to look for items where the graph of the rankings across management levels would show a rather smooth upward or downward slope, particularly where the differences are large and, therefore, the slope would be steep.

> At one company, product mix flexibility was ranked 5th in importance by top management, 9th at the plant-management level, 14th at the middle-management level, and 23rd at the supervisory level.

The number of these single slope relationships in a single data set may be an indicator of communication or consensus problems between top and lower levels of management. However, the critical issue is: are the patterns of ranks sensible?

An example of a sensible pattern of differences, a strategy/ tactic relationship, is shown in Figure 4–10. Here, the top level of management places significantly less importance on the performance factor "meeting production schedules" than the consistent very high importance placed on this measure at the lower management levels in the plant.

FIGURE 4–10
Levels Consensus—Strategy versus Tactics (Meeting Production Schedules)

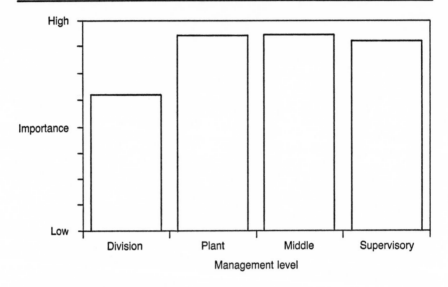

In followup discussions at this plant, it became apparent that all managers were concerned about on-time deliveries, but the tactic used internally to guarantee such deliveries by the second and lower levels of management was "meeting production schedules."

The juxtaposition of "meeting production schedules" with "on-time delivery" in Figure 4–11 bears out this explanation.

Still another example of consensus analysis is illustrated by Figures 4–12 through 4–19. This series of anomalies examines patterns across different functions in a company. They show a consistent difference between the perceptions of importance in one function and the perceptions in the other functions.

In this case, marketing seems dangerously unaware of the new directions in manufacturing and is unlikely to be able to use the new manufacturing muscle in this organization to any advantage.

The good news in the firm was that manufacturing was a competitive weapon; the bad news was that marketing did not know it!

FIGURE 4–11
Levels Consensus—Strategy versus Tactics (Meeting Production
Schedules—On-Time Delivery)

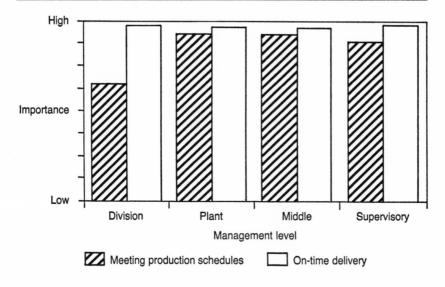

FIGURE 4–12
Consensus across Functional Areas (Labor Efficiency)

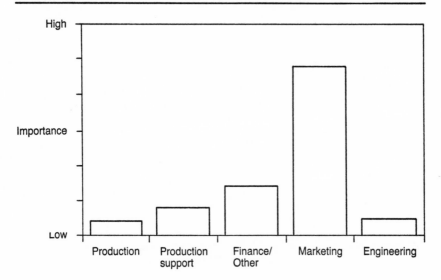

FIGURE 4–13
Consensus across Functional Areas (Machine Efficiency)

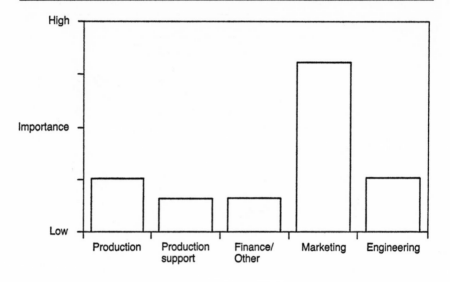

FIGURE 4–14
Consensus across Functional Areas (New Product Introduction)

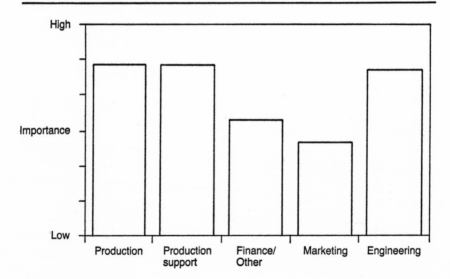

FIGURE 4–15
Consensus across Functional Areas (Manufacturing Throughput Times)

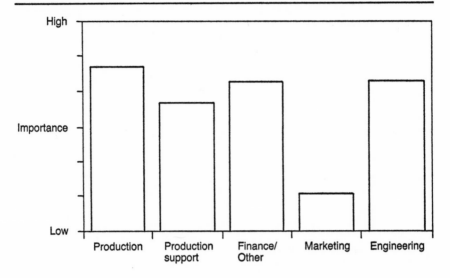

FIGURE 4–16
Consensus across Functional Areas (Integration with Customers)

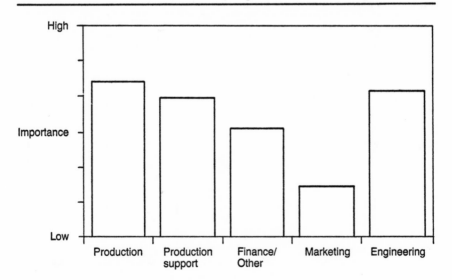

FIGURE 4–17
Consensus across Functional Areas (Cost Reduction: Dollar Savings)

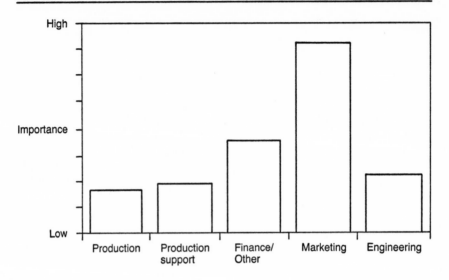

FIGURE 4–18
Consensus across Functional Areas (Unit Labor Cost)

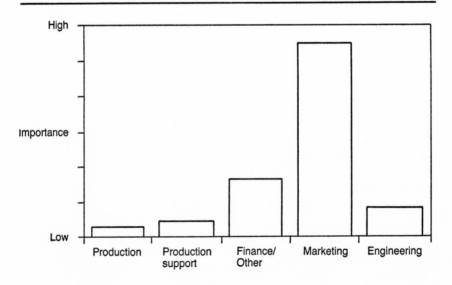

FIGURE 4–19
Consensus across Functional Areas (Direct Labor Productivity)

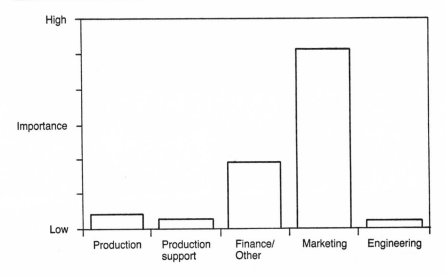

These data unleashed discussion among managers at the followup meeting and some serious overhauling of the education, training, and communication processes in the company.

A measure of the variability in the rankings across different functions or management levels can be used to aid in consensus analysis. Those items with the greatest variation across the rankings are the ones for which the least consensus exists. For example, the data in Figure 4–20 show part of an analysis for one company looked at across levels of management. In this case, a simple calculation of the standard deviation of the rankings on an item across management levels is used to indicate variability. This statistic is available as a function in most spreadsheet packages. The larger the standard deviation, the less agreement across levels.

> The standard deviation of the rankings highlights the improvement areas and performance factors on which there is strong agreement and major disagreement.

For example, there is consistency of opinion on the importance of "on-time delivery"—the ranks (1, 2, 2, 1) are close, and, consequently, the measure of variation is small. On the other

FIGURE 4–20
Variation in Ranks of Importance of Excellence across Management Levels

Performance Factors
Rank on Importance of Excellence

| | Level of Management | | | | Variation (standard deviation) |
Factor	Division	Plant	Middle	Supervisor	
On-time delivery	1	2	2	1	0.5
New product introduction	8	15	1	4	5.2
Meet production schedule	14	3	3	5	4.6
Vendor quality	6	10	4	2	3.0
Conformance to specifications	4	6	9	6	1.8
Safety	12	7	8	9	ı.9

hand, there is considerably more disagreement about "new product introduction"—the ranks (8, 15, 1, 4) are spread out, so the variation measure is much greater.

These measures of variation can be calculated for all analyses, by function as well as by management level. In the followup meetings, the interest often centers on which level or function appears to be odd man out.

Confusion Analysis

The final stage in the data analysis turns more directly to the variation in the responses.

> The goal of confusion analysis is to determine the relative extent of consensus in opinions on each improvement area and performance factor item within a group.

The "group" for confusion analysis can be any one of interest, from the entire set of respondents to any single function or level. In terms of the numerical analyses, confusion analysis provides a new set of ranking reports. This time, however, the standard deviations of the ratings are ranked instead of the means of the ratings. The resulting reports show the extent to which the respondents agree or disagree about the mean values determined for Parts II and III of the questionnaire.

As in the case of means, the standard deviation scores are ranked from largest to smallest. The largest values represent those items for which the greatest degree of confusion exists.

A typical item that almost always is near the top of the confusion list is CIM (computer integrated manufacturing). It appears there is little consensus on what this term means.

Several companies are inventing their own term for CIM, precisely so they can specify what is and is not included in the definition. This way, the understanding of the term is not greatly influenced by the choice of magazine one reads on the way to work.

An interesting reality check on the alignment analysis (the analysis by quartiles) described above is to see if the standard deviation rankings are low (relatively high agreement) for those items in both the top and bottom quartiles. Ideally there will be widespread agreement on what is most and least important. Figure 4–21 shows such an analysis.

Figure 4–21 is the same as Figure 4–3, except it now also includes the ranks for the standard deviations. High numbers correspond to relatively high levels of agreement and low number rankings are associated with more disagreement.

FIGURE 4–21

Top and Bottom Quartiles of Strategies and Ranks of Standard Deviations (in parentheses) at One Company Site

Strategic Action Areas Importance of Improvement			
Top Quartile		Bottom Quartile	
New product introduction	(24)	Job responsibilities	(9)
Customer satisfaction	(19)	Machine efficiency	(4)
Product technology	(23)	Direct cost reduction	(5)
Quality	(16)	Environmental control	(3)
Integration/customers	(22)	Labor efficiency	(1)
Manufacturing throughput times	(21)	Offshore manufacturing	(2)

The ranks for the top quartile are reassuring. "New product introduction" had the smallest standard deviation of the 24 left-side scores for the list of improvement areas, as shown by the 24 in parentheses. There was strong agreement that improvement in this area was important.

Throughout the top quartile, the rankings for standard deviations suggest consistent agreement across all respondents.

The ranks of the standard deviations for the bottom quartile's items show a lack of unanimity on the importance of these items. This might reflect the continued presence of the old measurement system.

While most people understand that measures like labor efficiency and machine efficiency are no longer significant, their retention in the system sends conflicting signals. This example dealt with the variation in answers from all respondents, but the same steps can be taken to check for confusion within levels or functions. However, this must be done with caution. Confusion analysis can be confusing. Fortunately, it is not crucial to do extensive confusion analysis. It plays a supportive role to the other analyses, providing background information only when and where it is needed.

Although confusion analysis does not always yield startling revelations, it occasionally identifies interesting questions for the PMQ review session.

EVALUATION AND CONSENSUS BUILDING

The most important part of using the PMQ occurs in the session where the results of the data analysis are shared with the questionnaire respondents.

The evaluation meeting for review of the PMQ analyses should have two fundamental objectives: creating commitment to changing existing performance measures, and developing an action plan for accomplishing the change.

It is usually not possible for all respondents to attend this meeting, but a wide representation of managerial levels and functions is important. It is particularly useful to have the key people who have the responsibility for implementing performance measurement changes, and who will have to live with the new metrics. It is vital to have the higher level managers there to participate, to learn, and to commit to change. Learning is what these sessions are about. Experience indicates there are always surprises, the reasons for the surprise results are often found through discussion, and the process helps develop a consensus in the organization for resolving problems.

The evaluative meeting typically takes a half day. Managers usually think it will be possible to do it in an hour or two, but this never happens. The meeting takes a fairly long time because the results are always provocative, and potential explanations for anomalies are numerous. It is difficult to know precisely how to orchestrate these sessions because there is a danger of becoming buried in the data. The emphasis should be on the most severe anomalies, across both functions and management levels.

Cooperation and teamwork are required (and should therefore be *managed*). Recriminations or the assignment of blame for particular results will derail the process. The discussion starts with a review of the questionnaire and its purpose. The focus then shifts to the alignment analysis and the match with corporate strategy. The next step is typically an investigation of the congruence between the measurement system and the organization's actions and strategies. The attempt is to build consensus about the measurements that need to be added or changed and those that should be dropped. Finally, one needs to turn to the areas where a lack of consensus between levels and functions appears to exist. This part of the discussion is often the longest and usually ceases only when the end of the day or unyielding flight schedules call a halt to the proceedings. However, the process does not end at this point; it should be just beginning.

There will be a need for a series of followup discussions, each one reaching more closure about what needs to be done and how to do it than the one before. We believe the role of consultants in this process needs to be significantly limited and curtailed over time. The important thing is for the organization to control the effort—without outsiders driving the process—and to carry it through to change.

If the questionnaire does not result in a change in performance metrics, the efforts will have been counterproductive. Before any firm decides to use this diagnostic tool, it needs to be prepared for change and committed to entering a process where change is anticipated at the end.

> The overall goal is embracing change.

This will play out differently in different companies, depending on their culture, history, competitive situation, and other factors. Each situation is unique; there are no "off-the-rack" problems or answers. Measures should plainly reflect strategies and tactics. Finally, it is imperative that measures should be deleted as well as added. In some cases, the deletion of an old measure may be more beneficial than the addition of any single new measure.

BENEFITS

There are several major benefits to the use of the PMQ. First, the data collected by the questionnaire identify both the need for and the demand for a change among managers, and they provide a catalyst for beginning the change process.

> Another benefit of the PMQ is that it provides a reality check on the perceived clarity and uniformity of the plant's mission.

One goal of this reality check is to ascertain the overall commitment to the mission. Another is to critically compare the collective opinion with the stated strategy of the organization.

The differences between the left-side scores and the right-side scores (the gaps and false alarms) show the extent of perceived mismatch between what is important and what the measurement system supports. The nature of the mismatch indicates whether a new measure needs to be added or an old one needs to be deleted.

> The PMQ provides access to the *real* performance measurement system, not the one on paper.

The real system is the one that influences what people do, the one they perceive. Thus, opinions are preferable to documents. An incident at one plant provides a good illustration. The company had a stated objective of reducing lead times and increasing material velocity. The company as well as the managers believed this also meant a reduction in importance in several of the classic accounting-based measures such as direct labor utilization and machine utilization. The questionnaire clearly showed this perception had not made its way through the organization. The lower level managers still were interested in the old measures, believed they were important for the company, and believed their performance was measured by them.

> The process of interpreting the results (the followup sessions) gets managers directly involved in the change process in a non-threatening way.

The ideas for change arise naturally, without being forced by a charge from the higher level of management, in part because the PMQ analysis localizes the specific areas where a change is needed and provides an avenue for evaluating the need for those changes. Additionally, PMQ fosters change because it is "our" numbers and opinions—not those imposed by someone else.

> The overall process of using the questionnaire provides an opportunity to help managers mentally cut the Gordian Knot.

This is a necessary prerequisite to any fundamental change in performance measurement systems.

CHAPTER 5

THE PERFORMANCE MEASUREMENT QUESTIONNAIRE IN ACTION: APPLICATION AT NORTHERN TELECOM

"The performance measurement questionnaire has given us insight into people's perceptions of our strategy-measures match-up. We're getting good information on both the gaps and the false alarms. What we have said is important in our strategy statement, the organization has taken to heart."

Robert Badelt
Director of Manufacturing
Northern Telecom Inc.

The Performance Measurement Questionnaire (PMQ) described in the previous chapter was constructed with the strategy-actions-measures model as a guide. It should be no surprise then that the PMQ proved useful in exploring the impact of an evolving manufacturing strategy on a performance measurement system. However, the PMQ was not merely a tool for observation. It played an active role in helping the people at Northern Telecom Incorporated (NTI) manage the changes in their performance measurement system necessitated by the implementation of a new manufacturing strategy.[1]

---

[1] For more information on the time-based strategy adopted at Northern Telecom, see Roy Merrills, "How Northern Telecom Competes on Time," *Harvard Business Review*, July–August 1989.

Several factors make the far-reaching application of the PMQ at NTI a particularly good demonstration both of the usefulness of the PMQ and of the effects of strategy changes on performance measurement.

First, Northern Telecom Inc. is close to the cutting edge in recognizing the critical competitive importance of finding appropriate ways to measure performance.

Observations from organizations with less awareness would not permit the same understanding of measurement system design implications.

Second, NTI has outlined and communicated to all of its units a comprehensive and comprehendible manufacturing strategy focused on satisfying the customer through time-based competition.

This eliminates a serious source of noise in cross-location comparisons. There may be variations across plants within NTI because of differences among the stages of strategy implementation reached by the plants, but the effect of NTI's central objectives should remain clear.

Third, the manufacturing sites included in this investigation at NTI all have very similar underlying technology.

All four plants manufacture digital telecommunications products. The basic knowledge required to build the products is very similar. However, the processes by which products are assembled do vary from plant to plant. Both traditional batch and JIT flow lines existed at the time the PMQs were used. Other, less radical differences also existed. Again, the basic similarity in technology allowed the performance measurement differences to be interpreted more cleanly.

In sum, while the similarities across plants reveal the fruits of a single competitive strategy, the differences reveal something about the ontogeny of implementing a performance measurement system to support that strategy. Four manufacturing plants and the U.S. headquarters were involved in the study. Perceptions about improvement areas and the performance measurement system were collected via the PMQ from about 35 managers at each location.

Additional observations were made at each site. These included unstructured interviews with people at various levels of management, direct observations of activity in both the factory and the office, and collection of objective facts about the site, its industry, its competition, and its personnel. Such information on the strategies and actions at the various locations was essential for placing the PMQ data in context.

STRATEGY AND ACTIONS

The four plant locations will be identified as plants A through D, the letters corresponding to the extent to which the corporate strategy has been implemented. Plant A was farthest along the path of strategy implementation, and Plant D was at the earliest stage at the time of the PMQ data collection.

Company Background and Manufacturing Strategy

Northern Telecom Inc. is the U.S. subsidiary of a global corporation that had its origins as Bell Telephone Company of Canada more than 100 years ago. NTI is organized into four administrative functions and four operating divisions. The functions can be characterized as technology planning, finance and administration, marketing, and strategic development. The operating divisions are switching, business systems (such as PBXs), transmission, and data communication/networks.

In 1986, NTI management recognized that growth had reached a plateau after years of expansion. This recognition led to a swift response. The focal point for growth revitalization was judged to be increased emphasis on innovation and responsiveness. A competitive advantage could be sustained from the rapid introduction, at mature quality and cost, of new products that met customer wants and needs. This premise became the cornerstone of a new corporate strategy. The strategy was elaborated to include:

> A critical role for manufacturing in the chain of events between product conception and market.

An emphasis on quality, service, and responsiveness in all functions to improve the new integrated view of the "product delivery process."

Concentration on activities that added value in this process and elimination of activities that did not.

It was believed that adherence to these priorities would yield market advantages that would result in revitalized growth. It was also believed that such growth could be achieved without material expansion of the work force if each function could find ways to vastly improve its throughput velocity.

NTI management recognized early that implementation of the new strategy in manufacturing would necessitate pervasive change in the organization. The extent of this change is illustrated by Figure 5–1, which was adapted from ideas formulated by Stanley Davis.[2] The concepts critical to the time-based competition strategy, shown in the upper-right-hand corner, were incompatible with the day-to-day culture in the factories. Conversely, the concepts in the lower-left-hand corner were highly consistent with the ongoing culture, but incompatible with the avowed strategy.

Achieving the desired match was recognized to be a large-scale undertaking—one that encompassed changing the basic culture and beliefs in manufacturing.

NTI further recognized that these changes would require clear communication, grass-roots education, and extensive training.

NTI also acknowledged that its traditional accounting-based performance measurement system was inappropriate.

For the manufacturing groups, ties to labor efficiency and absorption costs would interfere with achievement of the new objectives. However, the nature of the replacement metrics was unclear. At the headquarters level, a project was undertaken to move from the traditional, full-cost-based, profit-and-loss state-

---

[2]Stanley M. Davis, *Managing Corporate Culture* (Cambridge, Mass.: Ballinger Publishing Co., 1984).

FIGURE 5–1
**NTI's Analysis of New Manufacturing Strategy versus
Existing Corporate Culture**

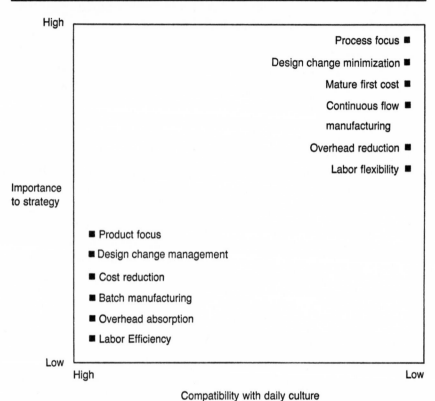

Source: Adapted from Stanley M. Davis, *Managing Corporate Culture*, (Cambridge, Mass.: Ballinger Publishing Co., 1984).

ment to one built on direct costs. At the same time, a decision was made to allow the operating divisions to determine for themselves specific new measures to employ at the plant level. This approach was congruent with the existing tenets of divisionalization.

In order to provide a central direction for development of new metrics, the corporate strategy document specified three top-down objectives:

- To improve customer satisfaction.
- To reduce overhead as a percentage of sales.
- To dramatically increase inventory turns.

The strategy document also specified criteria for assessing the objectives and established companywide action programs to achieve them. In the operations area, actions centered around just-in-time (JIT) and total quality control (TQC) programs.

Plant A

Plant A produces switching devices. It is unique among NTI's plants in that it is self-contained. All of the functions related to its product line (marketing, product R&D, manufacturing, finance and administration) are housed in one location.

Plant A's product line competes in a concentrated market, with few major competitors. The plant is relatively new. Although it is only the second-largest plant of the four, it employs the most people (due, in part, to its multifunction headquartering), produces the largest products, and requires the largest variety of material parts. The number of material part numbers at Plant A is 1.8 times the number required at the plant with the second-highest variety of parts. Despite this, it has the smallest number of suppliers among the four plants and nearly all of the suppliers are JIT/TQC qualified.

> NTI describes JIT/TQC qualification as a partnership with suppliers to "maximize their product and service levels, as well as their design processes and cost of quality."

A qualified supplier is fully approved on quality, reliability, timing of deliveries, and competitive price.

> Evidence of Plant A's success includes its dramatic increase in inventory turns, its twofold improvement in volume with no increase in personnel, an actual reduction in floor space requirements, and an amazing reduction in throughput time.

All production is organized into JIT flow lines. The plant has recently taken in some work from one of its sister plants to use some of the opened floor space. Its order-to-delivery promise time is about half the industry norm, and its actual production cycle time is significantly less than that!

These facts are impressive, but they cannot compare to the impression gathered from a tour of the factory floor. The work space is brightly lit, immaculately clean, and jarringly quiet. In fact, one's first impression is that almost no work is being done. The facts, however, belie that notion.

> Assembly workers are arranged into work cells. Each station is logically and ergonomically laid out. Even the chairs are state of the art. They are hydraulically dampened, with every conceivable kind of adjustable support.

An amusing, but not surprising, anecdote was told about envious managers trying to divert deliveries of these chairs to their own offices when they first saw them. The factory workers have better chairs than most managers!

Interviews found several floor workers to be both enthusiastic and knowledgeable about the full range of activities in their respective flow lines. This knowledge is no accident. It is the result of a serious and continuing commitment to education, training, and rewards at the plant.

Plant A trains, educates, and communicates with factory floor personnel through two main mechanisms. Broad-level education is achieved through regular classes run at the plant.

> Each person receives a minimum of 10 days' training and education each year. Furthermore, each functionally focused work cell is organized into quality circle teams (dubbed *employee involvement teams*). Each team, comprised of 6 to 12 individuals, meets daily.

Teamsmanship is a focus of the broad-level training, as is cross-skill training. Teamwork is fostered through other avenues, as well. Each team is encouraged to choose a team nickname and design a team logo. Each team maintains a "pride area" on the factory floor. These areas are comprised of several movable partitions and contain posted records of on-time production, daily defect counts, daily throughput, safety records and such, as appropriate to the team's activities. The teams determine what to display and maintain the records. They are encouraged to personalize these areas, with photos and cartoons, for example.

Further evidence of a climate that supported teamwork and cooperation are visible throughout the plant. Locally produced signs and banners celebrating customer service/satisfaction records, safety records (the plant is a state award winner in safety), and on-time deliveries hang both in the offices and above the factory floor. One huge banner displayed a horizontal list of the months of the year. Under each month's name was a number representing the percentage of shipments made by the promise date during the month. During a December visit, results for 11 months were posted. Each month had the figure 100 below it. This looked to be a good reason for another celebration.

Such results had regularly been recognized and rewarded with plantwide parties and cookouts. Team parties were also held to celebrate safety awards and the like.

> The predisposition toward celebrations is a distinctive characteristic of Plant A, one that contributes significantly to the plant's achievements and its ability to change.

These activities provide rapid recognition of accomplishments and make it clear that top management cares about what the teams do; the plant's top manager was almost always involved in the celebrations.

A long stream of 100 percent on-time deliveries does not seem to leave much room for improvement. Plant A management was aware of this and was searching for a more stringent measure of "on-time" that would better reflect what the customer wanted, not the quoted shipment date. The objective was to create an even better measure of customer service.

Plant A has one of the most impressive operations in the United States. It is important to note, given the present focus on performance measurement, that this model plant was not simply the product of a well-designed performance measurement system. The quality of the performance measurement system at Plant A has to be attributed to the environment in which it operates and its near seamless match to that environment. Three critical factors allow this plant to establish a good performance measurement system:

- The clear and simple mandate provided by the corporate strategy statement.
- The method used in the plant to engender grass-roots support for the new programs.

- The protecting position taken by the plant's general manager and the example he sets for his subordinate managers.

The vision provided by a strategy that specifically incorporates manufacturing as a cornerstone will, by its very presence, enhance the effectiveness of any performance measurement system designed to support it. The second and third critical factors identified above deserve further discussion.

Any performance measurement system, particularly one that is changing, needs the support and acceptance of the people operating under it. The management at Plant A was careful to create an environment in which change was regarded positively before attempting to modify attitudes, beliefs, and behaviors.

One crucial step in the process at Plant A was to dedicate time each day to cleaning up the factory and improving its general appearance and comfort level. Each individual, manager or worker, was responsible for the plant in general, as well as his or her own "neighborhood." Walls were painted, floors were cleaned and polished, lines were painted to designate traffic areas, and lighting and ventilation were improved.

> These activities emphasized people and the proper working environment over immediate output. It became obvious that the right work would be achieved, but achievement would come by attending to the needs of the people and the processes for performing the work.

Another step in this process was to educate the work force (including managers) to the benefits of TQC and JIT methods. Once the education programs were in place and the first flow lines were being installed, supervisors and their teams were given responsibility and authority for design and layout. The lines were theirs and the results were theirs. This redoubled interest in seeing things work well.

> In short, the plant began to employ the employees' minds as well as their hands.

The last critical factor cited above was the role played by the plant's general manager. At the time the corporate strategy was implemented at Plant A, the corporate performance measurement system was still basically driven by traditional financial measures. The general manager of the plant took a stance that demonstrated his faith in the strategy, in his managers' conversion of that strategy into tactics within the plant, and in the ability of the other employees to successfully convert those tactics into improved performance.

This stand did not lack significant risk. *He* was still evaluated against the old measures. Senior management with years of experience and success under the old metrics had a difficult time ignoring the old signals. A couple of examples clarify how this stand was demonstrated.

A recently automated section of one of the flow lines included a new machine. Because of the constant advances made in streamlining the line, however, the new machine had already become a bottleneck in the process. One of the production managers indicated it was going to be replaced at significant cost despite it newness.

> The cost justification for this change was not a problem: none was needed. The mandate was to reduce throughput time and increase inventory turns. Within the plant, this was all that mattered.

Replacement of the machine would reduce throughput time. However, the dollar amount in question was sure to be noticed at headquarters, and if the improvements did not accrue in the near term, the plant manager could have egg on his face.

In another case, the manager in the plant with the most seniority presented the general manager with a traditional budget on which he had spent many hours over several months. Due to the man's savvy about the way the old system worked, the budget would have produced good indicators for his department. When he took the budget into the general manager's office to present it, the general manager tore it in two and tossed it into the wastebasket without even looking at it.

> The effort involved in generating the budget, the general manager told him, was at odds with the new strategy. It did not directly address the new objectives. Such budgeting (as opposed to planning) was an overhead activity that did not add value!

The subordinate realized, after he got over the shock, that the general manager was serious about making the new measurement system work. The subordinate, like a reformed smoker, is now one of the plant's leading advocates of JIT and TQC.

The three critical factors described above can be characterized as top-down mandate, bottom-up groundswell, and managerial umbrella holding. They are necessary ingredients in the metamorphosis to a different performance measurement system.

Plant B

Plant B produces business systems. The primary marketing group and the R&D group for this product line are located elsewhere. Price competition for Plant B's products is stronger than that faced by Plant A. Plant B has more than twice as many customers as Plant A and more than twice as many major competitors, each of which competes globally.

The plant was only about eight years old at the time, but had already been expanded twice. It is the largest of the four plants, although it employs slightly fewer people than Plant A. Plant B has the smallest variety of material parts, less than one third of the variety at Plant A. However, it has two thirds more suppliers, of which less than 20 percent are JIT/TQC qualified.

Plant B would compare favorably to most operations in its industry, despite being outshined by Plant A. The plant is well-lit and cleaner than most. It varies in terms of noise level and elegance of layout. The safety level is very good and is a major focus. Each of the three flow lines produces a different group of items. The one dedicated to a relatively few high-volume items is the most developed. The others are dedicated to wider varieties of lower volume products.

Plant B's management has made a significant investment in training with a focus on quality and JIT concepts during the past few years. At the same time, a conscious effort was made to develop a team orientation.

The plant's top managers perceive that these actions have enhanced their ability to implement change. The resistance to change has decreased because people are better able to understand the reasons for change, and they feel more involved in the process.

Plant C

Plant C is one of two plants described here in the access-transmission group. Plant C does fabrication and final assembly. Research, development, and marketing are located nearby in a separate facility. Plant C faces five major competitors in a highly competitive market. The market is comprised basically of 20 major customers.

Plant C was in its ninth year of operation at the time of writing. It is two thirds the size of Plant B, and employs five sixths the number of people. The variety of parts required by Plant C falls midway between the numbers for Plants A and B, but the number of suppliers is approximately the sum of the numbers for those two plants. Even this large number represents a 40 percent reduction over previous years. Much of the reduction in the number of suppliers is attributable to a vendor qualification program. About one third of Plant C's suppliers are JIT/TQC qualified.

An obvious focus at Plant C is safety. Touring the plant, one cannot help but notice the frequency and variety of posted safety records, banners, and the like. Such tokens easily outweigh those devoted to quality or customer service. Like Plant A, the plant is organized into quality circle teams that hold debriefing meetings daily. Many of the aforementioned safety notices were designed by individual teams. These signs all point to a more inward focus at Plant C. This is consistent with the stage of manufacturing strategy implementation there.

Plant C had just begun the installation of JIT flow lines. As a consequence, plant layout was only fair in comparison to Plants A and B. Cleanliness and noise were also more of an issue than in those plants.

A theme of change was clearly present at Plant C. In addition to the advent of JIT and flow lines, the plant manager recently left after a new director of access was appointed. That director had temporarily assumed the duties of plant manager as he waited for one to "grow" from within Plant C.

Furthermore, the managers had just completed a first round of training on JIT techniques and philosophy. As at Plant A, this training was 10 days per year. At the time of our visits, worker training was focused on basic skills because a large block of new workers had just been absorbed into the work force.

Plant D

Plant D is another plant from the access-transmission group. Among the four plants, Plant D is the only one for which no direct external market exists. Its sales consist entirely of supplying (at transfer prices) demand from 10 other NTI plants. Nonetheless, the plant is operated as if under strong competition. Plant D's existence was threatened if outside vendors could better meet NTI's requirements. Low-cost production was a definite priority. The plant manager, in tune with NTI's corporate strategy, defined the plant charter as building quality products in minimum elapsed time and at minimum cost.

Plant D uses about the same variety of parts as Plant B, half as many as Plant C and slightly more than one quarter of the number used by Plant A. However, it has the largest number of suppliers and none of them are JIT/TQC qualified for Plant D in particular. The factory is the smallest one of the four we visited and has the smallest work force. The plant was in its sixth year of operation.

> Factory floor attention is largely focused on cost savings. Workers are paid a bounty for their cost savings suggestions. This is an area of concern to plant management, which views the program as incompatible with a JIT/TQC philosophy.

As JIT is implemented, this program will have to be dismantled and replaced. However, because the program has been so heavily emphasized, plant management recognizes the importance of achieving grass-roots support for such a change.

The plant has a confusing layout consisting of various work

areas with a maze-like path meandering through it. Every inch of floor space seems to be in use. JIT approaches were not in evidence during our visit, but were said to be planned. Floor management and workers were receiving two basic types of training: cross-skill training and teamsmanship training. Training intensity was six days per year.

At the time, department meetings were held weekly. Ergonomics teams met weekly to discuss work area layout and compatibility. This activity seemed to focus on safety and productivity. All the banners and signs on the floor appeared to be official issue and not homemade as seen in the other three plants. There were no department pride centers.

PERFORMANCE MEASUREMENT QUESTIONNAIRE

"This is something we need to go back and do maybe once a year or every other year. For a general manager or an operations director, it has a lot of value."

Robert Badelt
Director of Manufacturing
Northern Telecom Inc.

The PMQ was used at each of the locations to collect data about managers' perceptions of the performance measurement system. A total of 174 managers at the five NTI sites filled out the questionnaire. For each of these sites, a detailed examination was conducted, using alignment, consensus, congruence, and confusion analysis, as described in Chapter 4. The details of these analyses are too massive to be discussed here. Instead, the discussion here focuses on the overall NTI data, comparing the different sites, rather than the management levels or the functions within the sites.

Each factory is viewed as a unique entity, with its own measurement problems. Companywide measurement change issues and the need to eliminate some traditional metrics crystallize under this view.

Alignment Analysis

Alignment analysis starts with the left-hand side of Part II (the improvement areas). When the managers' responses are averaged across all respondents, the eight areas regarded to be most important to improve are (in order from most important):

Customer satisfaction
New product introduction
Integration with customers
Education and training
Product technology
Quality
Manufacturing throughput times
Process technology

At least seven of these eight items appeared in the top eight at each of the five sites. All of these improvement areas are consistent with the corporate strategy focus on time-based competition. Table 5–1 shows the top quartile for each of the five locations as well as the overall results.

Looking at the between-plant similarities and differences tells something not only about the effectiveness with which the corporate strategy has been implemented at the plants but also about the effectiveness of the PMQ in capturing that information. Plant A's most serious differences at the top with other sites is that education and training ranks ninth and product mix flexibility ranks seventh.

> Because Plant A has the most extensive education and training program, its relative lower importance ranking for improvement in this area seems appropriate. Also, Plant A is the most experienced in JIT flow lines. Thus, the importance of flow line "bandwidth" has risen.

Mix flexibility averages about five places lower in importance to improve at the other plants.

Plant B has no major differences with the overall set of responses at the top of the list. Because it represents the mid-point

TABLE 5–1
Top 25 Percent Strategic Importance of Improvement in Area
(Most Important First)

Plant A	Plant B
New product introduction	New product introduction
Customer satisfaction	Customer satisfaction
Product technology	Education and training
Quality	Integration with customers
Integration with customers	Quality
Throughput times	Product technology
Plant C	**Plant D**
New product introduction	Integration with customers
Customer satisfaction	Customer satisfaction
Integration with customers	New product introduction
Education and training	Education and training
Throughput times	Integration with suppliers
Process technology	Process technology
Headquarters	**All Sites**
Customer satisfaction	Customer satisfaction
New product introduction	New product introduction
Integration with customers	Integration with customers
Quality	Education and training
Education and training	Quality
Product technology	Product technology

among the plants studied in terms of strategy implementation, this is not surprising.

> What is impressive is the consistency across sites and the match between the perceived importance areas and the focus of the corporate strategy. The message seems to have been communicated well.

Plant C also matched the overall pattern. The only difference other than some ordering differences in rank positions five through eight is the presence of integration with suppliers in the seventh position. This is the major difference at Plant D, too, where integration with suppliers occupies fifth place. The whole pattern of placement across plants in terms of importance of improving integration with suppliers serves as an acid test of the questionnaire.

Because JIT/TQC techniques require integration with suppliers, the importance of improvement should vary inversely with the degree to which such techniques are (successfully) in use. Thus, going from Plant A to Plant D, the importance ranking of this area should rise. In fact, it does, with Plants A through D ranking it 14th, 9th, 7th, and 5th, respectively.

Another interesting feature of this data subset is the list of areas least important to improve. Table 5–2 recaps the lowest quartile of improvement importance rankings for the five sites.

Three traditional cost-based performance measures appear near the bottom of the list: direct cost reduction, machine efficiency, and labor efficiency.

Again, the pattern of rankings is consistent with the level of strategy implementation. Labor efficiency appears within the

TABLE 5–2
Bottom 25 Percent Strategic Importance of Improvement in Area
(Least Important First)

Plant A	Plant B
Offshore manufacturing	Offshore manufacturing
Labor efficiency	Environmental control
Environmental control	Labor efficiency
Direct cost reduction	Inventory management
Machine efficiency	Procurement
Job descriptions	Job descriptions
Plant C	**Plant D**
Offshore manufacturing	Offshore manufacturing
Labor efficiency	Labor efficiency
Environmental control	CIM
Job descriptions	Environmental control
Direct cost reduction	Direct cost reduction
Performance measurement	Job descriptions
Headquarters	**All Sites**
Offshore manufacturing	Offshore manufacturing
Labor efficiency	Labor efficiency
Direct cost reduction	Environmental control
Environmental control	Direct cost reduction
Job descriptions	Job descriptions
Machine efficiency	Machine efficiency

lowest three rankings for all plants. Because labor efficiency is the first old metric to go in a JIT environment, this makes sense. Machine efficiency is given the lowest perceived importance among the four plants at Plant A, the highest (a ranking of 14 out of 24) at Plant D, and rankings about halfway between these extremes at the other two plants. These results directly reflect the stages of JIT/TQC implementation.

A quick review of the responses concerning the importance of excellence in the performance factors confirms the overall impression cast by the improvement area analysis. As shown in Table 5–3, the constituents of the top quartile are consistent with the strategy of customer-oriented, time-based competition.

> When viewed across sites, there is not perfect agreement on the top and bottom quartiles for performance factors, but overall the rankings are remarkable more for their agreement than for their differences.

The greatest disagreement in the top quartile of rankings of performance factors is for sales forecast accuracy. Plant A assigned a rank of 22 to that performance factor, while the other three plants gave it much higher importance.

TABLE 5–3
Left-Side Performance Factors All Plants Plus Headquarters

Top Quartile	Bottom Quartile
On-time delivery	Direct labor productivity
New product introduction	Unit labor cost
Vendor quality	Environmental monitoring
Meet production schedule	Variances
Conformance to specifications	Minimizing environmental waste
Safety	Number of material part numbers
Yields	Number of suppliers
New model introduction	Capacity utilization
Sales forecast accuracy	Dollars shipped per period
Vendor lead times	Indirect labor productivity

The management at Plant A has recognized that forecast accuracy diminishes in importance when it has much shorter lead times than its competitors.

Forecasting is a difficult task that seems only to be getting more difficult in our increasingly dynamic economy, so committing resources to improvement in manufacturing response time rather than to creating more sophisticated forecasting techniques is a rational solution.

One final issue particularly well addressed in alignment analysis is a comparison of results achieved at NTI with those of other companies. PMQ has been applied in many other situations, but the results have never demonstrated the level of consistency and uniformity seen at NTI. One cannot help but conclude this result is the effect of a straightforward corporate strategy that specifically identifies objectives for manufacturing.

Congruence Analysis

A major part of congruence analysis is finding the gaps and false alarms. As explained in Chapter 4, a gap exists when the measurement system is not properly supporting some necessary improvement action. In those cases where the measurement system supports improvement significantly beyond its level of importance, false alarms exist.

Table 5–4 provides the top quartile of the difference measure (left hand minus right hand) for the improvement areas, on a site-by-site basis.

Three of the four plants and headquarters rated new product introduction as their biggest gap. Thus, support of new product introduction is the most important measurement problem facing NTI.

The second biggest gap occurs in integration with customers. Plant D rated it as the biggest gap. Plants B and C rated it third. Plant A rated it 15th. Recall that Plant A had made this a priority and had been measuring it.

TABLE 5–4

Gaps in Performance Measurement System Support for Strategic Action Improvements (Largest to Smallest Gaps)

Plant A	Plant B
New product introduction	New product introduction
Product technology	Information systems
Overhead cost reduction	Integration with customers
Integration with suppliers	Process technology
Performance measurement	CIM
Information systems	Education and training

Plant C	Plant D
New product introduction	Integration with customers
Customer satisfaction	New product introduction
Integration with customers	Integration with suppliers
Integration with suppliers	Volume flexibility
Product mix flexibility	Product technology
Throughput times	Product mix flexibility

Headquarters	All Sites
New product introduction	New product introduction
Integration with customers	Integration with customers
Quality	Product mix flexibility
Product mix flexibility	Integration with suppliers
Education and training	Product technology
Customer satisfaction	Customer satisfaction

At the other end of the spectrum, Table 5–5 is the bottom quartile for the difference measure, the false alarms. For example, direct cost reduction, labor efficiency, and machine efficiency are on the list of false alarms at Plant A. Measures of these items still existed at the plant, despite a nearly universal recognition that improvements in these areas would not lead to better health for the firm. The clear implication for Plant A management was to remove those obsolete measures.

Because direct cost reduction, labor efficiency, and machine efficiency are on the false alarm list for headquarters, and the first two are on the lists for the other plants, it now may be possible to eliminate these measures from the entire corporate culture.

Table 5–6 presents the top and bottom quartiles for the performance factors, but only for the overall (all sites) analysis.

TABLE 5–5

False Alarms in Performance Measurement Support for Strategic Action Improvements (Largest to Smallest False Alarms)

Plant A	**Plant B**
Direct cost reduction	Offshore manufacturing
Offshore manufacturing	Labor efficiency
Environmental control	Inventory management
Labor efficiency	Environmental control
Machine efficiency	Direct cost reduction
Inventory management	Throughput times
Plant C	**Plant D**
Offshore manufacturing	Offshore manufacturing
Labor efficiency	Environmental control
Environmental control	Direct cost reduction
Direct cost reduction	Labor efficiency
Job descriptions	Performance measurement
Performance measurement	Job descriptions
Headquarters	**All Sites**
Direct cost reduction	Offshore manufacturing
Offshore manufacturing	Labor efficiency
Labor efficiency	Direct cost reduction
Inventory management	Environmental control
Machine efficiency	Inventory management
Manufacturing strategy	Job descriptions

TABLE 5–6

Gaps and False Alarms in Performance Factors at All Five Sites (Largest to Smallest in Both Cases)

Performance Factor Gaps	Performance Factor False Alarms
Sales forecast accuracy	Dollars shipped per period
Number of engineering changes	Unit labor cost
New product introduction	Direct labor productivity
Vendor quality	Cost reduction: dollar savings
Change/setup times	Variances
Vendor lead times	Departmental budget control
Number of material part numbers	Margins
Indirect labor productivity	Inventory turnover
New model introduction	Dollars of capital investment

The overwhelming predominance of cost-based measures on the list of false alarms clearly supports the need for NTI to eliminate these measures in the evaluation of manufacturing performance.

The gaps in both Tables 5–4 and 5–6 are heavily weighted toward areas that are both important for a customer-oriented, time-based strategy and difficult to quantify. It is common for measurement systems to support best those areas that are most easily quantified.

As competitive strategies evolve, priorities that resist numerical definition are becoming more important.

Finding ways to measure and manage these priorities will be one of the major challenges facing leading companies as they become world class manufacturers.

Consensus Analysis

Consensus analysis across the five sites is concerned with the differences in perceptions across the sites for particular improvement actions and for detailed measurements. In general, the consensus analysis is remarkable for the broad agreement across NTI plants as to what is most and least important to improve and to measure. However, in the analysis shown in Table 5–7, Plant A stands out from the others in the improvement area differences, on which the greatest cross-plant disagreement exists.

Plant A's superiority in implementing the manufacturing strategy clearly gives it a different set of priorities for improvement. The plant has already accomplished better integration with customers, resulting in relatively less need to improve customer satisfaction.

The unique "new priorities" for Plant A are also highlighted by this analysis: performance measurement, quality, and product technology.

In all three of these areas, Plant A has a significantly higher ranking for the difference between needed improvement and the extent to which existing performance measures support improvement in that area.

TABLE 5–7

Rankings of Improvement Area Differences (Left Hand-Right Hand) Top Quartile of Greatest Disagreement (Largest First)

Improvement Area	Headquarters	Rank of Difference between Importance and Support at:			
		Plant A	Plant B	Plant C	Plant D
Performance measurement	13	5	17	19	20
Product mix flexibility	2	15	3	3	1
Quality	3	7	10	18	12
Customer satisfaction	6	16	12	2	8
Procurement practices	15	9	18	7	17
Product technology	14	2	9	11	5

Confusion Analysis

Several approaches could be taken to confusion analysis, the most straightforward being to calculate standard deviations using the entire data base of 149 respondents. However, the consensus analysis based on sites as the unit of analysis clearly indicates there are major differences among the sites, and the differences are largely attributable to the different implementation stages of the manufacturing strategy. As such, any combined analysis may be misleading.

> The bottom-line conclusion is that each of the four plant sites has its own set of unique problems and opportunities, and each is at a different evolutionary stage in implementing the manufacturing strategy.

Each plant will require some tailoring of its performance measurement system to reflect individual differences in what is being achieved. On the other hand, it is also important to emphasize the large degree of congruence in metrics that is seen across the NTI organization:

> There are more things that are the same than different, and many performance measures can be standardized across plants with quite different challenges facing them.

CONCLUSIONS

> "Overall, the questionnaire can give you a lot of insight into what's going on in your organization."
>
> Robert Badelt
> Director of Manufacturing
> Northern Telecom Inc.

The administration of PMQ at four different operating sites and the corporate headquarters of NTI provided several important insights into changing performance measurements.

> The individual plant assessments provided focus for each of the factories as they were reviewing their performance measurement systems.

In every case, the evaluation meeting produced a consensus on directions for changing performance measures and a set of concrete action plans. There was also considerable interest generated in the results at other plants, and particularly in the results at the corporate level. The evaluation meeting for the headquarters group produced a mandate to eliminate many financial-based measures, as well as an understanding for the need to work more closely across functional areas.

> The overall effort provided considerable insight to overall NTI manufacturing, both in terms of what is important and in the extent to which the strategy is working.

Interactions with the managers during the actual administration of the questionnaire and at the followup sessions supported the impression that PMQ provides insights into the appropriate measurement problems. Despite and because of the relative simplicity of the statistical methods applied to the data, the questionnaire results clarified for managers which measurement areas presented the greatest barriers and opportunities in manufacturing.

> Conducting the study in the multiple NTI sites clearly provided for the examination of strategy implementation on performance measurement.

It is probably dangerous to generalize too freely about the relationship between strategy changes and measurement from a single set of observations, but it appears that successful implementation of the new strategies requires a reallocation of the emphasis placed on measures.

> The strategy change was the driver for measurement change in the NTI case, though it is not apparent that the process is entirely one-sided.

In other words, implementation of the new strategy was clearly fostered because the measurement system also evolved. Had the measurement system remained static, further implementation of the strategy would have been blocked.

> The final benefit of the multisite administration of the PMQ is that it provided a foundation for generalization about performance measurement based on more rigorous analysis.

CHAPTER 6

BALANCING FINANCIAL AND NONFINANCIAL MEASURES OF PERFORMANCE

The question "what's wrong with cost accounting?" implies traditional cost accounting needs to be fixed to make it applicable to measuring performance for the new competitive realities. Cost accounting systems can be improved, but incorporating the right nonfinancial measures in the performance measurement system provides more immediate benefit and holds greater long-term promise in today's dynamic business environment. The strategy-actions-measures interaction dictates the use of both financial and nonfinancial measures. The mix is shifting toward *more* nonfinancial metrics, although financial or accounting-based measures are still widely used. The critical issues are:

- *When* and under *what circumstances* are financial measures appropriate?
- *When* and *where* should nonfinancial measures be used?

Finding the right mix of financial and nonfinancial measures is dependent on several critical dimensions:

- The use of financial measures as a function of the level in the management hierarchy.
- The use of financial measures as a function of the market stability in which the products compete.
- The use of financial measures as a function of the extent to which the process technology is integrated.

For each of these dimensions, it is possible to assess the balance between financial and nonfinancial metrics exhibited in the data from Northern Telecom. It is also useful to review some lessons from the literature. Then, suggestions for the design of performance measurement systems can be made.

In Chapter 2, it was argued that cost accounting traditionally has served three purposes in organizations, the main of which was to support financial reporting to outside groups. Controlling factory operations has been another traditional use for cost accounting data. Unfortunately, for performance measurement, the measures are typically too irrelevant due to allocations, too vague due to "dollarization," too late due to the accounting period delay, and too summarized due to the length of the accounting period.

Several other ideas have been introduced that have further bearing on the applicability of financial performance measures. Among these are the ideas of contingency, continual improvement, strategic versus maintenance measures, the strategy-actions-measures connection, and the combined top-down and bottom-up change implied by the whole person concept. These ideas have been supported by company examples, including two major manufacturers that have shifted factory performance measurement systems away from financial measures.

However, the firms have not abandoned financial performance measures at higher levels in the company; even at lower levels, financial measures have not been uniformly abandoned. The question this raises is whether the firms are just slow to make a complete break with financial measures, or whether their approaches are simply appropriate for their situations. Analyses of the facts and of the literature supports the second alternative: differential use of accounting-based measures reflects different needs and different questions for different problems.

USE OF ACCOUNTING MEASURES AS A FUNCTION OF ORGANIZATIONAL LEVEL

It seems that managers talk more and more like accountants the higher they are in the organization. Although a cynical view might lead one to conclude that this is the result of a country club mentality (that is, managers who talk like accountants promote only subordinates who talk like accountants), such an explanation does not appear to match reality. A better explanation for this phenomenon is that accounting-oriented measures make more sense as the manager's level in the organization rises. This is true because the problems, concerns, and actions are fundamentally different at a top management level than they are for day-to-day operational control.

The actions taken are more long term in nature, dealing with underlying problems as opposed to symptoms.

The actions taken deal with larger parts of the firm, where summary measures are more interpretable than masses of detail.

The length of the accounting period is consistent with the frequency with which results are reviewed.

Dollarization is the only way disparate operating units can be compared.

Perhaps, overhead allocations are seen in their proper context—as a useful way to consider plans and options, but as much less useful for evaluating past actions.

The NTI Data Viewed in Terms of Management Level

The fresh data analysis presented here is limited to the data gathered from the 149 managers at the four operating plants of Northern Telecom. Recall that the Performance Measurement Questionnaire (PMQ) has two sections that ask managers about their perceptions of performance measures. Part III presents a list of potential measures and asks managers to indicate how important each is to the long-run survival of their company and the extent to which the company emphasizes each measure. The ratings are based on the managers' perceptions of importance, not the (possibly inappropriate) formal system of measures.

Data from Part IV of the questionnaire are also analyzed. Part IV is the free response section, where managers are asked to name the measure they believe best describes the primary measure of their own performance for each of daily, weekly, monthly, quarterly, and annual time frames.

Figures 6–1 and 6–2 show the structure of NTI responses that appear when the managers' responses are partitioned into top, middle, and lower management, corresponding to the standard hierarchy of strategic, tactical, and operational control.

Both figures illustrate the same relationship between management level and the usefulness of accounting-based performance measures.

> Financial performance measures are seen as having more importance and primacy at higher levels of management than at lower levels.

This relationship makes sense. Decision time horizons are much longer at the strategic level than they are at the operational level. The definition of *timely* responses varies accordingly. Thus, the time lag inherent in cost-based feedback is less troublesome at higher management levels. The control process at higher levels of the organization needs to be preprogrammed to a much lesser degree than at lower levels, where the focus is more on immediate responses to concrete problems.

While control at lower levels can be seen as similar to the

FIGURE 6–1

Financial Measures as a Percentage of Top-Ranked Measures by Management Level

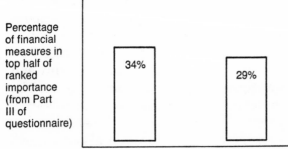

Percentage of financial measures in top half of ranked importance (from Part III of questionnaire)

34%   29%   25%

Strategic   Tactical   Operational

Management level

FIGURE 6–2
Financial Measures as a Percentage of Named Top Measures
by Management Level

control provided by a thermostat, at higher levels the comparison cannot be made. A thermostat, sensing a drop in temperature, turns on the furnace. This type of response at the lower levels of management is less likely to be signaled by financial measures than by nonfinancial ones such as quality levels. The thermostat analogy is not appropriate at higher levels of management where alarm signals lead less to actions than to analysis of underlying causes.

It is enlightening to examine the literature on feedback and control in view of these results. A short digression involving some ideas from cybernetics, the science of control, is in order.

Lessons from the Literature

William Ross Ashby, a prominent cyberneticist, captured a fundamental idea in his Law of Requisite Variety.[1] It states that, in order to have effective control, a system must have a variety of

---

[1]William Ross Ashby, *An Introduction to Cybernetics* (London: Chapman and Hall, 1964).

responses equal to or greater than the variety of disturbances it faces.

Two basic strategies can be used to create the required variety capacity in a control system. One is reducing the variety of disturbances, which can be achieved by simplifying and systematizing the processes to be controlled. A thermostat-driven heat system works when other sources of variation in temperature are held to a minimum. Thus, the area to be heated should be sealed and insulated, and the response of the heating system immediate and reliable. Given these conditions, the thermostat can provide good control. But the reduction in the variety of disturbances is more important to heat control than the thermostat itself. A reliable heater with no thermostat can usually provide more desirable control than a reliable thermostat with no heater.

The other way to create variety capacity is to increase the variety of responses. According to Ashby, this can be most efficiently done through a hierarchical arrangement of feedback systems. As stated above, in business, the hierarchical levels are often described as operational control, tactical control, and strategic control. In cybernetics terminology, they are called *first-, second-,* and *third-order feedback.*

First-order feedback controls are feedback systems of the thermostat type. The characteristic that identifies them as first-order is that there is a single, invariant triggering measure.

Second-order feedback involves regulating a regulator. Operations are controlled with reference to criteria that are *changed* as the environment, goals, or structure of the system change. To extend the thermostat analogy, a multiple setback thermostat, where the regulated temperature is dependent on a timer with several settings, illustrates a second-order feedback system. The budgeting process also exemplifies second-order feedback in an environment where manufacturing variances are used. Based on a review of prior year results, current goals and strategies, and a forecast of the environment, specific standards (criteria) are defined. These new standards redefine the activation points for (first-order) cost variances. More sophisticated forms of second-order feedback involve changing the nature of the control criterion. For example, observed changes in the competitive environment might lead to a change from the use of cost of rework measures to feedback on percent first-pass yields.

Third-order feedback is goal changing and strategy identification. It is the reflective process of strategic planning. First-order feedback can be viewed as *having* a solution. Second-order feedback reduces to *choosing* a solution. In comparison, third-order feedback requires knowing how to *generate* solutions.

Measurement System Design Implications

The three levels of feedback described by cybernetics map very nicely onto the hierarchy of management in organizations. The performance measurement system should provide different kinds of feedback loops at each level of management. At each level, the feedback should be action-oriented and timely, but the nature of the actions differ from level to level as does the definition of *timely changes*.

At the lowest level of management, the feedback mechanism should elicit immediate operational solutions. At the middle-management level, performance measurement should elicit changes in operational procedures or focus. That is, performance measurement should result in changing the criteria for the next level down, selecting new solutions. At the strategic level of management, performance measurement should elicit corrections in choice of strategies to meet goals. Such changes in strategy cascade through the lower levels of control, identifying what needs to be solved at the middle level and, eventually, resulting in operational control employing new solutions.

Against this background, it is easier to see why accounting-based performance measures make more sense at higher levels of management. For the lowest level of management, feedback should indicate whether the activities are being performed correctly. The relationships need to be direct. Thus, nonfinancial measures such as schedule and quality performance are more appropriate. This does not mean financial measures have no place. But they will make up only a minority of important measures. Wang's measurement of waste in financial terms is an example.

Cost variances, as derived from a standard cost accounting

system, do not provide direct feedback on correct performance. Cost variances are passengers, not drivers. They produce summary *results* of activity and yield information about the performance of activities only to the extent that the overall plans for the company are working; in most cases, the causes for deviations and the corrective actions are not revealed directly. For financial measures to be useful for operational control, the system has to be simple and regular *and* the relationships between actions and costs have to be stable. However, the simple, regular, and timely operational control systems defined by the survey responses rarely involved financial measures.

Simple and regular systems follow the first approach to control advocated by the Law of Requisite Variety: reduce the variety of ways that things can go wrong. If an organization can find simpler, more regular ways of manufacturing, the feedback aspect of control can be achieved by measuring the few important things that such simplicity makes obvious. These few important things are likely to be direct, nonfinancial measures of competitive priority actions, like first-pass percentage, on-time delivery, or cycle time. Thus, measures can be defined in the same units by which corrective actions can be taken and can be collected in time increments that support quick response to problems.

Additionally, a stable relationship between actions and costs is, in itself, not very desirable. If learning to produce faster, smarter, and better leads to lower costs, then a goal of stable action-cost relationships *hinders* this learning! An important implication is that continual improvement or learning is not compatible with cost-based measures used at the operational control level. Increasingly, embracing change will be required. New strategic measures will be added, and older measures relegated to the status of maintenance measures. Limiting measurement signals to financial terms represents a large barrier to the identification of improvement actions and fails to underscore the need for changes in actions.

At the middle-management or tactical level, the measures should indicate when a change in approach is needed to meet the overall strategy. Such a task is, by its nature, not highly programmable. The feedback signal needs to indicate which actions are not working, so new actions can be selected and controlled. Here, costs, to the extent that they measure the effectiveness of tactics, might provide such signals. Even here, however, basic manufacturing cost variances and measures of labor productivity are not likely to be of much value. Middle managers should be selecting measures that lead to improved learning or improvement in basic operations. That is, the measurement systems should highlight two critical issues:

- How good is the appraisal of the basic operational activities?
- How can the appraisal process be sharpened—that is, how can the measurements be improved?

Feedback for the middle managers should reveal whether selected measures are leading to simpler, faster, smarter, better manufacturing. In some cases, accounting-based maintenance measures may be fine for such a purpose. For example, inventory turnover may be a check on the success of nonfinancial measures related to process simplification, cycle time reduction, or even education and training.

Even less programmable is strategic-level feedback and correction activity. At that level, the objective of the feedback signal is to indicate when a change in strategy is necessary to reach the organization's goals. Such a signal may emerge when financial goals are not being achieved despite the successful pursuit of a strategy. In a sense, top management, when setting strategies, is defining hypotheses about how to reach goals. Because most organizations have important financial goals, it seems appropriate that those hypotheses are tested against financial results. If a strategy relates to improved financial performance and better market penetration based on processing velocity, then market share and return on investment might be good criteria.

But it is important to make reality checks against the strategic goals as well as the lower level objectives. A common example of mismatch is seen where a manufacturing firm does a magnificent job of achieving material velocity through just-in-time and other action programs, but does not have products attractive to the customer. In order to reach the desired bottom-line financial results, it is time to change the strategy, the measures, and the actions—to refocus on what will achieve the marketplace objectives.

Many firms believe introducing more new products and reducing new product introduction time will lead to market leadership, which in turn will lead to financial spoils. In those cases, financial measures such as total margins for new products and the percent of total revenue coming from products with a life of X months or less might be useful criteria, in addition to the more direct nonfinancial measures.

The characteristics of the potential financial performance measures discussed above still do not call for traditional cost accounting-based manufacturing variances. Rather, summary or aggregate measures are likely to signal the need for a change in strategy or tactics, while specific financial measures can be useful indicators of progress. Measures such as inventory turnover, cost of quality, margins and return on investment are more likely to be among the list of appropriate potential measures.

To recap, there are three major implications of these findings, each of which requires firms to cut the Gordian Knot:

1. Controllable operations need to be simple and regular and their performance needs to be measured in terms of corrective actions, typically in nonfinancial terms.
2. Financial performance measures are more useful at higher levels of management, where they reflect the success of action plans or of strategies.
3. Although costs, by definition, add up from individual activities to firmwide totals, performance measures have to make sense on *other dimensions*!

USE OF ACCOUNTING MEASURES AS A FUNCTION OF MARKET STABILITY

In the immediate postwar era, when traditional, accounting-based performance measurement was at its zenith, competition was dominated by price and dependability issues. Production was oriented to long, low-cost runs, so the relationships between action and resultant cost could be identified. Labor costs made up a much larger share of value-added cost, so cost meant labor and labor utilization indicated the actions to be controlled.

Cost-based performance measurement made sense then in terms of the thermostat requirements of real-time feedback and preprogrammed responses, too. Long, efficient production run manufacturing resulted in a wide timeliness window. It also defined long periods of mature production, where the emphasis was on maintaining standards, that is, the status quo, not making improvements. Moreover, to the extent that improvement was desired, it was against the same units of measure, not new problems. The preprogrammed response was "do what you did before."

In this era of increasing market dynamism, traditional cost-based performance measures are less and less appropriate. Thus, a finding that nonfinancial measures are perceived to be of relatively more value when product life cycles are short is not surprising. Other features of a dynamic market environment produce a similar conclusion.

The NTI Data Viewed in Terms of Market Stability

In Figures 6–3 and 6–4, the managers' responses are grouped into two categories according to whether their plants' products compete in stable or dynamic market environments. Plant B is the only one classified as being in the dynamic environment category. The life cycles for its products are much shorter than those of the products manufactured at plants A, C, and D. Plants C and D make products based on older technology, and the markets in which they compete are dominated by price and quality considerations. Plant A's products are technologically advanced, but competition in that market, at the time of the data collection, was still based on price and dependability, as it had been for many years.[2] On the other hand, Plant B manufactures prod-

---

[2]Interestingly, Plant A may change the nature of competition in its market, since it seems to have a competitive edge in terms of rapid response time and minimal required lead times for both dependable delivery and installation.

FIGURE 6–3

Financial Measures as a Percentage of Top-Ranked Measures by Market Stability

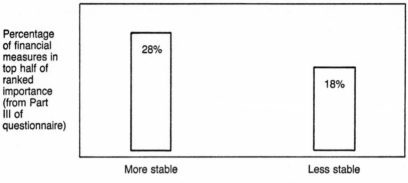

Percentage of financial measures in top half of ranked importance (from Part III of questionnaire)

More stable 28%

Less stable 18%

Competitive market stability

FIGURE 6–4

Financial Measures as a Percentage of Named Top Measures by Market Stability

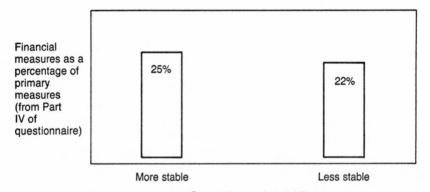

Financial measures as a percentage of primary measures (from Part IV of questionnaire)

More stable 25%

Less stable 22%

Competitive market stability

ucts that compete on innovative features and vendor responsiveness and support.

Both graphs evidence the same pattern:

Accounting-based financial measures are considered more important in plants where the market environment is stable.

This relationship echoes the findings of several previous studies on the comparative appropriateness of accounting-based control systems.

Lessons from the Literature

Several studies of accounting-based control and performance evaluation systems and their effects on performance have reached the same conclusion:

Accounting measures are more appropriate, in terms of positive effects, where the competitive environment is less uncertain, where the basis of competition is less complex, or where the business unit is implementing a more predictable "harvest" competitive strategy rather than a more uncertain "build" strategy.[3]

Govindarajan was involved in two studies that revealed similar relationships to the ones suggested by the graphs in Figures 6–3 and 6–4.[4] In one study, he partitioned data into more and less effective performance groups. For the more effective group, he found an association between increasing environmental uncertainty and decreasing use of accounting-based performance evaluation. In the other study, co-authored with Gupta, the strategy-environment connection was explored. In environments where a harvest strategy was effective, nonaccounting

---

[3]See, for example, Gordon and Narayan, "Management Accounting Systems, Perceived Environmental Uncertainty, and Organization Structure: An Empirical Investigation," *Accounting, Organizations and Society* 9, no. 1 (1984), pp. 33–47.

[4]V. Govindarajan, "Appropriateness of Accounting Data in Performance Evaluation: An Empirical Examination of Environmental Uncertainty as an Intervening Variable," *Accounting, Organizations and Society* 9, no. 2 (1984), pp. 125–35; and Govindarajan and A. K. Gupta, "Linking Control Systems to Business Unit Strategy: Impact on Performance," *Accounting, Organizations and Society,* 10, no. 1 (1985), pp. 51–66.

performance evaluation actually hampered effectiveness, while nonaccounting performance evaluation was found to contribute to effectiveness in environments characterized by high growth, where build strategies were more effective.

Several other studies also reflect the same basic relationship:

> Accounting-based measures of performance make more sense in relatively stable competitive environments.

When managers view the competitive environment as complex or uncertain, nonfinancial measures of performance make more sense.[5]

Measurement System Design Implications

The patterns of perceived importance and analysis of the data in Figures 6–3 and 6–4 reflect a relationship between the usefulness of accounting performance measures and the nature of the competitive environment. Although it does not show *which* specific measures are useful, it does provide some guidance as to which kinds of measures are likely to make sense in a given market situation.

> More importantly, both the literature and the data analysis indicate that if market stability is changing, the relative use of financial-based measures needs to change accordingly.

Because most organizations with any history are likely to have a relatively large share of their performance measures based on accounting data, the advent of increased uncertainty or unpredictability in an organization's markets signals a need to change the measurement system—almost surely toward the use of more nonfinancial measures. According to the strategies-actions-measures notion, this is also likely to mean that actions need to be changed or have changed, as well.

---

[5]See, for example, D. C. Hayes, "The Contingency Theory of Managerial Accounting," *The Accounting Review*, January 1977, pp. 22–39; or P. Brownell, "The Role of Accounting Data in Performance Evaluation, Budgetary Participation, and Organizational Effectiveness," *Journal of Accounting Research*, Spring 1982, pp. 12–27.

The central implication here is that organizations that wish to grow and thrive are going to have to face the fact that they need to change both their actions and their measures to the extent that their market environment changes. There is growing evidence that almost all firms realize their market environments are becoming more uncertain. This can be seen in the growing deterioration of the quality of sales forecasts. An informal poll of several thousand manufacturing managers has turned up less than one manager in 2,000 who believes accurate forecasts will become easier to achieve in the future.

> The global economy seems to be moving toward time-based competition. Production responsiveness of competitors will improve. New product, new model, and new process introduction rates are increasing. These trends foretell a time in the *near* future (if not already) when performance measurement systems based solely on accounting data will be obsolete. The eventual survivors are cutting the Gordian Knot and learning to change their performance measures now!

USE OF ACCOUNTING MEASURES AS A FUNCTION OF PROCESS INTEGRATION

Production is organized into many single-process or single-function departments in traditional companies. This is the "divide-and-conquer" approach, where the manufacture of products involves sequential passage through many discrete production departments, including separate departments for functions such as inspection. Typically, there are buffer stockpiles of in-process goods between these departments. The emphasis is on utilization of the separate departments or processes, not on the timely flow of materials through the process conversion steps. A similar mentality is seen at a higher level in organizations where work units are organized in functional silos.

In more and more firms, this approach is being replaced with one where work activities are organized around flows of materials, flows of new products, or other flows that cross organizational boundaries. In this integrated process approach, activities such as inspection and material handling are often performed by the same people that perform manufacturing operations. The emphasis in job responsibilities is on general skills, not specialization. One specific example of the difference in orientation is seen in the distinction between JIT/flow lines and traditional departmental, batch-oriented manufacturing.

As in the case of market stability, a relationship between the degree of process integration and the usefulness of accounting performance measures makes sense in both historical and logical terms. The time period in which cost-based performance measures were used without much complaint was also the time period in which differentiated approaches to assembly-type manufacturing were dominant. In today's environment, where a variety of integrated approaches to assembly-type manufacturing are gaining favor (for example, continuous flow lines, focused factories, integrated work cells), cost-based performance measures are being decried as inadequate.

The NTI Data Viewed in Terms of Process Integration

For this analysis, the NTI data can be partitioned according to managers using flow line manufacturing concepts and those that are not. In this case, the former are Plants A and B, while the latter (nonflow line) has Plants C and D. This partition is not as clean as it might be, however, because some plants have invested much more heavily in flow line concepts than others. This partition, moreover, only considers integration in terms of producing products. Plant A also is more highly integrated in terms of product design than the other three plants.

Grouping responses to Parts III and IV of the questionnaire along the line of differentiated versus integrated manufacturing processes produces the results shown in Figures 6–5 and 6–6.

In the sets of responses from Part III data, Figure 6–5, there is a clear contrast in terms of the perceived importance of financially based performance measures.

> Financial measures seem to be considered more appropriate under traditional divide-and-conquer process approaches than under integrated flow line approaches.

FIGURE 6–5
Financial Measures as a Percentage of Top-Ranked Measures by Technology

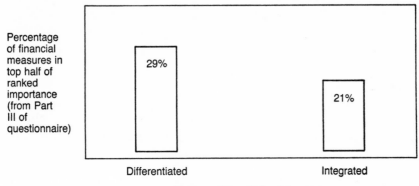

Percentage of financial measures in top half of ranked importance (from Part III of questionnaire)

29%   21%

Differentiated   Integrated

Process differentiation/Integration

FIGURE 6–6
Financial Measures as a Percentage of Named Top Measures by Technology

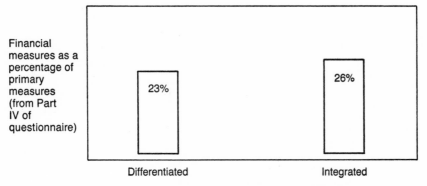

Financial measures as a percentage of primary measures (from Part IV of questionnaire)

23%   26%

Differentiated   Integrated

Process differentiation/Integration

However, in terms of the Part IV data illustrated in Figure 6–6, the relationship is reversed, although the difference is not as dramatic. Historical trends, the logic of the situation, and the formal statistical analyses are all consistent with the relationship illustrated in Figure 6–5. Thus, the pattern in Figure 6–6 is, at first, puzzling. This anomaly underscores the complexity of balancing financial and nonfinancial performance measures.

Probing further, two factors that affect the appropriateness of accounting measures of performance have been identified: management level and competitive environment. Each of these dimensions is buried in Figures 6–5 and 6–6. We cannot peel off these effects except through statistical methods, which show results paralleling Figure 6–5. However, we can show this comparison within a single level of management. Figure 6–7 depicts the relationship for the operational level of control only. The pattern matches that in Figure 6–5! The source of the reversal can be traced to structural differences (Plants C and D have fewer upper middle managers, who are likely to use more financial measures) and to differences in competitive environments across the plants.

FIGURE 6–7
Financial Measures as a Percentage of Operational Managers'
Named Top Measures by Technology

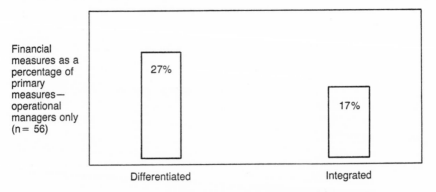

Lessons from the Literature

In a sense, cost accounting tradition has recognized that differences in manufacturing systems along the dimension of process integration call for different measurement techniques. This is exemplified in the textbook distinctions between job order costing methods and process costing methods. However, studies of this relationship are few and difficult to relate to each other or, directly, to the NTI data.

One study that deserves mention was conducted by Daft and MacIntosh.[6] Their experiment demonstrated that a determinant of the success of a management control system was the fit between the quantity and ambiguity of data and the type of task technology employed by the organization. Later work by MacIntosh builds a strong case for believing that what he calls craft and research technologies, where the means to an end are not well understood or analyzable, require multiple-focus ambiguous feedback.[7] The idea is that this will allow the manager to discover, or intuit, the pertinent corrective action.

> In the case of routine or technical-professional technologies, feedback should be focused and unambiguous so the corrective action is preprogrammed or determinable through deliberation and analysis.

Admittedly, neither Daft and MacIntosh nor MacIntosh speaks directly of the differences between traditional and flow line manufacturing, but the parallels between job-order processing and craft technology and between focused factories and routine technology are compelling. Neither do they speak directly of financial and nonfinancial measures, but it is easy to argue that accounting measures provide multiple-focus feedback, while focused feedback with preprogrammed responses requires nonfinancial, action-oriented measures.

---

[6]R. Daft and N. B. MacIntosh, "A New Approach to the Design and Use of Management Information," *California Management Review*, Fall 1978, pp. 82–92.

[7]N. B. MacIntosh, "A Contextual Model of Information Systems," *Accounting Organizations and Society* 6, no. 1 (1981), pp. 39–53.

Measurement System Design Implications

It appears that accounting-based performance measures are less well-suited to environments where the emphasis is on integrated flows. This is so regardless of whether the integration is around traditional work flows as is the case in just-in-time manufacturing, better new product introduction procedures that cross functional silo boundaries, or better integration with either suppliers or customers.

Increasingly, leading edge firms are turning to these kinds of activities to achieve new competitive advantage. More and more firms realize the payoffs are in the connections of routine manufacturing to upstream and downstream activities. To the extent that firms view improvement in these connections as strategically important, their measurement systems need to reflect the changes. Evidence indicates that accounting-based measures will decrease horizontal compatibility. In fact, typical financial measures encourage within-unit actions that ignore the effects on inter-unit coordination!

> If the trend to more integrated modes of manufacturing continues, including customer-supplier partnerships and cooperative joint ventures, performance measurement systems based primarily on accounting data are likely to be valuable to a diminishing number of manufacturers.

This is still another reason for Gordian Knot cutting and developing the organizational climate that embraces change.

PUTTING IT ALL TOGETHER

Analysis of the NTI data, lessons from selected writings, and observation of trends in manufacturing companies all point to some guidelines about when, where, and how to use (and not use) accounting-based measurements. These guidelines do not define a new system of measurement, but they do address a number of the contingencies confronting managers.

The goals to which a performance measurement system should be addressed are, ultimately, the strategic goals of the organization. Therefore, a performance measurement system must have alignment between strategies and measures. However, such a connection is not, of itself, sufficient for defining an effective and efficient feedback system. The operational connection between strategies and measures is through actions! A good performance measurement feedback loop should elicit actions that lead to strategic improvement. Thus, the more physical the performance being controlled, the more action-specific the measures should be. In all cases, performance should be measured to complement the real time of the corrective actions.

> Performance feedback for correction works best when the sources of variety in the monitored activity are minimized and the corrective actions are well-focused on the remaining sources of variation.

Based on the analyses in this chapter, one would expect organizations facing the most unstable competitive environments and integrating their manufacturing processes most to be the ones most dissatisfied with traditional cost-based performance measures. There is evidence that this is the case.

As mentioned in Chapter 2, a recent survey of manufacturers conducted for the NAA and CAM-I showed that executives in the electronics industry, an industry characterized by highly dynamic competition and large shifts to integrated manufacturing processes, expressed significantly more dissatisfaction with accounting performance measures than the average for the survey. Furthermore, a recent study found that several minicomputer and microprocessor manufacturers facing highly dynamic markets and employing integrated flow lines and JIT principles for assembly did not even allow middle and lower level manufacturing managers to see manufacturing cost reports because they were believed to introduce too much irrelevant information. In one case, this policy was formulated by the company's controller and chief financial officer.[8]

The combination of observations, evidence cited by others,

---

[8]Judith A. Harris, *A Field Study Examining the Structure and Substance of Cost Accounting Systems,* Unpublished Doctoral Dissertation, Boston University, 1988.

and the analysis of the NTI data present a compelling argument for generalizing the relationships presented in this chapter. Accounting-based performance measures become less useful as:

- The market environment in which the firm competes becomes more dynamic.
- The internal processes through which products and services are produced become more integrated.
- The level of management at which performance is being measured becomes more operational and closer to physical production activity.

What do these relationships imply for manufacturers? First, the effect of global, time-based competition will be more dynamic markets for everyone. Furthermore, as discussed in Chapter 1, the trend to more integrated modes of manufacturing, including customer-supplier partnerships and cooperative joint ventures, will continue.

> This suggests *everyone* needs to learn how to change performance measures. The sooner they learn, the more of a competitive advantage they will have.

The second major implication comes from the relationship between measures and management levels.

> Organizations need to recognize that performance measures do not need to (indeed, probably *should* not) add up and down across functions and management levels.

Performance measures at each level should logically lead to performance at the next level up, but they do not have to meet mathematical requirements of additivity and exhaustiveness.

> Additivity may not enhance performance, but when all the numbers add up and balance, it feels like all is right! Casting this idea aside truly requires cutting the Gordian Knot.

The last major implication is a bit more subtle. The usefulness of financial performance measures varies as other characteristics of a firm's situation vary. Thus, this argument is directly against the notion that there can be a single right way to measure performance.

Each organization, each unit within each organization, and each unit within each organization at each point within its strategic, market, and technological evolution will require its own unique set of performance measures. This does not mean there should not or cannot be great similarities in measures across organizational units or across time. It does mean, however, that learning to change measures, and learning to change them better and faster, is going to be an important competitive skill for manufacturers in the future.

CHAPTER 7

DESIGNING PERFORMANCE MEASUREMENT SYSTEMS

Peter Murray, vice president of operations for Amalgamated Machines, and Barbara Friesner, director of operations, were discussing how Amalgamated could continue to improve performance and become even more competitive. Great strides had been made since Barbara had questioned performance measurement as the manager of service part sales. Revamping the measurement system led to significant changes in Amalgamated's actions. A number of production centers had been converted to flow lines, and everyone was pursuing quality improvement. Performance on on-time delivery, defect rates, customer satisfaction, market share, and productivity were better than ever. The question that concerned Murray and Friesner was, "What next?"

"What next?" is a critical question facing every manufacturing company. Is it new strategy? A different set of actions? New measures? The right answer is undoubtedly "All of the above," and whichever element of the strategy-actions-measures triad is addressed first, measurement issues will arise repeatedly. For Murray and Friesner, the desire to extend their successful quality improvement program may lead to the question of *how to incorporate continuous improvement explicitly into their measurement system,* the topic of the first major section in this chapter. Given the emphasis on quality programs by North American manufacturers, this issue is of particular interest.

Once that quest is accomplished, they, and managers in many other manufacturing firms, may turn to the task of assessing their flexibility. Murray and Friesner will find themselves confronted by a concept with which they have little experience. Yet, business scholars in both Japan and Europe suggest the competitive battles of the next decade will focus on flexibility, so savvy managers need to know how to position their companies on that dimension. The second section of this chapter provides a starting point for *understanding manufacturing flexibility and measuring it.*

Regardless of whether Murray and Friesner choose to pursue continuous quality improvement, flexibility, or some other new strategic goal, they must design their measurement system to support its attainment. The final section in this chapter, and this book, reviews *the attributes of measurement systems and their design that support pursuit of the new competitive priorities.*

CONTINUOUS IMPROVEMENT

Companies like Amalgamated may be pleased by evidence of improvement, but they should not be satisfied until their measurement system can tell them the improvement is both rapid and ongoing. Improvement by itself is not sufficient; companies do not compete against their historical performance. They contend with other companies that are also improving. Over the long run, the rate of improvement determines whether an action program will create a competitive advantage.

Learning-Based Measures at Analog Devices

One of the more innovative and effective approaches to incorporating continuous improvement into the measurement system and to creating congruence between strategy, actions, and measures can be found at Analog Devices Inc., a firm with headquarters in Norwood, Massachusetts, and with manufacturing locations around the globe. Analog competes in the data acquisition market, selling monolithic and hybrid integrated circuits for military, avionic, and computer applications. Its 1988 revenues of approximately $440 million were split evenly between foreign and domestic sales.

> Analog's sales of linear integrated circuits is one of the few electronics products in the United States with a positive balance of trade with Japan. Its market share is continuing to grow there.

Analog's goals for the next five years are ambitious; it wants to continue to increase sales at 20 percent annual rate, almost twice the rate of growth in its customers' markets. Analog intends to achieve this goal by being rated number one by its customers in total value delivered. Obviously, however, this is just the tip of the iceberg. Many internal improvements must be made to enable the company to penetrate its current markets further and to develop new markets.

> The performance measurement system is playing a major role by driving Analog toward continuous improvement in several key competitive dimensions.

The new measurement approach at Analog is being driven from the top down, under the guidance of Arthur Schneiderman, the director of quality/productivity improvement, and of the Corporate Quality Improvement Process Council, comprised of Analog's top management. The council establishes the objectives for the quality improvement process, determines the training methods to be used, monitors progress, and sets the reward structure.

> Analog has a formal quality improvement process (QIP), which is, in essence, the "actions." The effectiveness of the process in various divisions is evaluated with the performance measurement system.

The competence of the quality improvement process is judged using a group of nonfinancial measures reflecting the company's performance as viewed externally and internally.

Division management is evaluated on four external measures:

1. On-time delivery performance.
2. Defects in shipped materials measured in parts per million.
3. Lead time.
4. Number of unique product features.

The internal performance measures, that is, factors the customer does not directly observe, are:

- Time to market for new products.
- Yields.
- Manufacturing cycle times.
- Defects detected during manufacturing in parts per million.

In the quarterly performance summaries, these measures receive equal billing with the four financial measures:

1. Sales.
2. Sales growth.
3. Contribution.
4. Return on assets.

All of these measures are reported on a single page, which includes a summary of performance over the previous year. Giving nonfinancial measures equal status with financial measures at this level of aggregation is noteworthy, but it is not this characteristic that makes the Analog performance measurement system stand apart from others.

The Half-Life Concept

Schneiderman's use of the concept of the half-life makes Analog's measurement system a driver of continuous improvement. A half-life measurement identifies a rate of reduction, the amount of time it takes for half of the thing being measured to disappear. The thing can be radioactivity, as in the most familiar use of the idea, but it can also be ice cream or defect levels.

The underlying concept is that any defect level, if measured and systematically attacked with a goal of improvement, will decrease at a constant rate.[1]

This approach results in an ability to express any measure of defect improvement as a function of the time it takes to cut the difference between the current defect level and the theoretical minimum in half. Schneiderman calls this the half-life for improvement. For example, the original cycle time for production of a part is 11 hours. The theoretical minimum cycle time is 1 hour. A cycle time improvement effort on that part is initiated, and one month is required to reduce the cycle time to 6 hours. In this case, it took one month to cut the excess cycle time, 10 hours, in half, so one month is the half-life. In another month, the cycle time would be reduced to 3.5 hours, assuming the improvement process is maintained. Figure 7–1 shows the approach, as applied to two sets of actual data by Schneiderman.[2]

In his article, he applies the model to 64 sets of data that have been published in quality improvement articles. In each case, he calculates the half-life for improvement, the number of improvement cycles the data represent, and the amount of variance explained by the regression line that best fits the data set.

The analysis leads to the conclusion that the model fits well in the vast majority of cases.

---

[1]When the defect rate is plotted on semilog paper against time, the result will be a straight line, with the following mathematical form:

$$Y - Y_{min} = (Y_0 - Y_{min})^{-a(t - t_0)/t_{1/2}}$$

where:

Y = defect level
Y_{min} = minimum achievable defect level
t = time
t_0 = initial time
a = ln 2
$t_{1/2}$ = defect half-life

[2]Arthur M. Schneiderman, "Setting Quality Goals," *Quality Progress*, April 1988, pp. 51–57

FIGURE 7–1
The Half-Life Concept: Empirical Examples

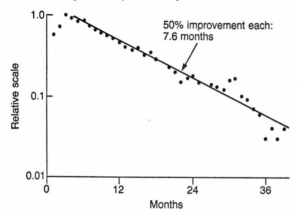

Eastman Kodak Copy Products Division
Average defects per unit, all products

50% improvement each:
7.6 months

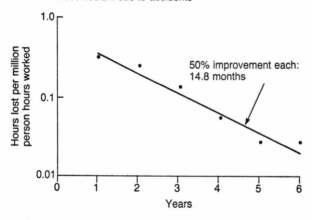

Japan Steel Works, Ltd., Hiroshima Plant
Absenteeism due to accidents

50% improvement each:
14.8 months

Source: Arthur M. Schneiderman, "Setting Quality Goals," *Quality Progress*, April 1988, p. 55.

Schneiderman uses the term *defect* in a general sense. He is not restricting it to errors or yield losses; it includes inventory, absenteeism, late deliveries, setup time, order lead time, and all varieties of cycle times.

Either the observed or the normative half-life for the improvement process can be used to establish goals for future periods. Schneiderman proposes the half-life lengths displayed in Table 7–1 as starting points for setting appropriate goals. These are based on his analysis of the published data sets. It is interesting to see that improvements that cross boundaries are much more difficult to achieve.

Schneiderman believes the length of an improvement half-life is closely related to the number of functions involved in the process, with fewer functions leading to faster learning and shorter half-lives. Thus, an improvement process applied within a single function has the shortest expected half-life, in the zero-to six-month range. A process involving not just multiple functions, but also multiple entities, such as two companies or a company and a government agency, generally leads to much longer half-lives, reflecting the added complexity of coordinating activities across organizational boundaries. The half-lives Schneiderman proposes are derived from his analysis of many quality improvement processes in a variety of companies and industries. When experience indicates improvement can be attained more rapidly or less quickly, the goals can be adjusted accordingly.

> The half-life *itself* becomes a performance measure—one that explicitly tracks continuous improvement.

To track a division's performance against its goals, Analog uses an approach to statistical quality control charting. Results

TABLE 7–1
Proposed Half-Life Model Values

		Months	
Project Type	Examples	Model Half-Life	Range
Unifunctional	Throughput	3	0 to 6
Cross-functional	New product cycle	9	6 to 12
Multi-entity	Vendor quality	18	12 to 24

are posted on a chart with three lines drawn on it, an example of which is shown in Figure 7–2. The center line represents the anticipated path of improvement, determined from a regression of the actual data. The exterior lines mark the boundaries of acceptable variation away from the goal, based on the variability of the actual data around the regression line.

Figure 7–3 is a set of actual data for eight separate areas at Analog. The performance is for the percent of scheduled lines due but not shipped on time. The data are always displayed for one year (12 data points). Any data point outside the control limits for the previous four months is displayed as a cross (+) instead of a triangle ($\triangle$). In actual use, the data are plotted in color, with positive control chart variations displayed in green and negative in red.

Division managers with results falling outside these control limits must explain why, regardless of whether the deviation has

FIGURE 7–2
Sample Half-Life Performance Measurement

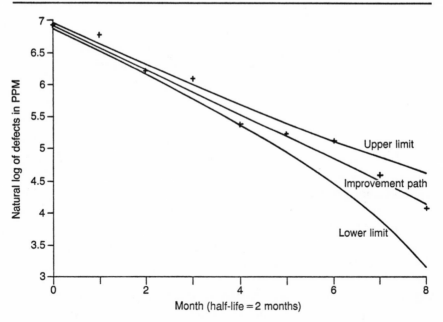

FIGURE 7–3
Half-Life Experience at Analog (Customer Service Performance-August 1987 through July 1988)

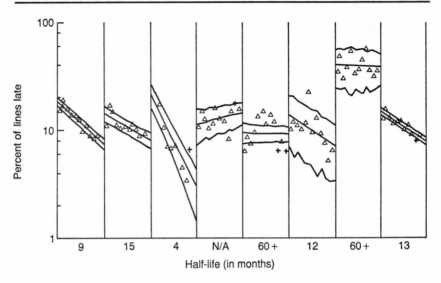

been positive, that is, more rapid learning than expected, or negative.

> The assumption is that variations are due to assignable causes. The manager's first responsibility is to understand the forces at work in production. Woe to the manager who does not know the cause.

The point is that learning must be continuous. If a division has discovered an effective way of solving some problem, it is important to articulate that approach and share it with other divisions. When a division is making little or no improvement, management must be able to determine what the barriers are so they can address and overcome them. The typical bottom-line reason is that the QIP process is not working as it should.

Continuous Improvement

Although Schneiderman's quality organization has been responsible for the majority of development in the measurement system at Analog, the success of the system is attributable to support from a wider range of sources. The division managers at Analog have embraced this measurement approach enthusiastically and find in it a basis for constructive competition.

> The half-life concept provides a common denominator by which performance can be compared across divisions, and the scorecard, the one-page display of measurements, has rapidly become an anticipated part of the operations reviews.

Another important source of support for the measurement change at Analog is the computerized management information system. The measures are made available on the computer almost immediately at the end of the reporting period. In other words, the information is available when it still has relevance. Further, the system is gradually expanding to provide background information for the highly aggregated division results. This enables division management to dig into the data to identify the sources of the results.

This contrasts with the situation in a performance measurement pilot project at a large, highly diversified manufacturing firm. The task force in that pilot program was very successful in identifying new measures that supported their JIT initiatives. By collecting the measures manually for a number of months, they demonstrated the superiority of those measures to the traditional numbers. However, more than a year after the successful demonstration, the divisional information systems group continues to refuse to collect the new measures on the computer. The reprogramming requirements are deemed too great. At Analog, the process is being driven from the top down, which helps explain why the systems people have supported putting the new measures onto the computer.

The iterative nature of the relationship between actions and measures is clear in the Analog example. Actions, the quality improvement process (QIP), drive development of the nonfinancial measures, but, in turn, the half-life measures lead to initiation, expansion, or elimination of actions. Measures cause changes in actions. The half-life measures identify areas where improvement is lagging, leading to implementation of new actions. In turn, when the actions succeed in pushing improvement along the desired path long enough, the necessity for measurement may be reduced to the maintenance level. At that point, the number and frequency of measures may need to change again.

Speculating on the pathway this change process may follow is intriguing. To date, the focus has been on quality and service. Improvement in these drivers has supported a steady reduction in costs. Some would argue this progression is predictable, and the next iteration of "what next?" will lead to a shift in focus toward flexibility.

FLEXIBILITY: THE NEXT COMPETITIVE BATTLE?

Several years ago, Professor Jinchiro Nakane visited Boston University. At a meeting with academic colleagues and industrial practitioners, they discussed the "focused factory," and the idea that one needed to pick the basis on which one wanted a factory to achieve excellence. The standard choice is between quality, dependability (that is, customer service), cost, and flexibility. Professor Nakane stated that Japanese companies did not see this as a tradeoff; firms need to achieve all of these priorities, but they need to tackle them in the order listed above. First, one needs to attain good quality. Then one should be able to manage customer delivery without problems. Then the manufacturing company needs to work on cost reduction. Finally, the company, having achieved excellence in the first three competitive priorities, can attack flexibility.

The worldwide *Manufacturing Futures* data offer ample evidence that many Japanese manufacturers are now working on flexibility as their number one competitive priority. Furthermore, they do not perceive flexibility to be in conflict with any of the other priorities.

> Quality, dependability, and cost excellence are simultaneously maintained, while flexibility is pursued.

The former priorities are reflected in maintenance measures, while flexibility is followed through strategic measures.

The pursuit of flexibility is easily seen by a comparison of the data among the three regions of the world. Japanese manufacturing firms are ahead in the introduction and use of flexible manufacturing systems (FMS), programs to reduce lead times in manufacturing, improved new product introduction processes, setup time reduction, and expanded job definitions for all workers. These trends are also seen in North America and Europe, but the relative ranked importance given to them is significantly less.

Manufacturing firms in the United States and Europe are necessarily catching up in the basics of quality and dependability.

Also, data indicate Japanese firms are paying more attention to upstream manufacturing activities. The emphasis given to CAD/CAM in the survey results is only one indicator. More telling evidence is provided by discussions with several North American manufacturers that compete directly with Japanese companies. These companies have made the startling realization that their Japanese competitors can get a new product from inception to introduction in *one half* the time it takes their own firms.

Meeting the flexibility challenge requires a clear understanding of the various dimensions that comprise flexibility. Management must be able to determine the strategic aspects of flexibility in order to provide overall direction to the evolution of both the manufacturing infrastructure and the measurement system by which it is to be evaluated.

A Flexibility Framework

A crucial step in thinking about flexibility is to do so in strategic terms and to establish a common vocabulary. One of the greatest barriers to understanding the construct has been the lack of consistency in references to manufacturing flexibility.

Flexibility in the definition of *flexibility* is not a virtue.

In the most general sense, flexibility is an organization's responsiveness to change; the changes are generated both by external and internal forces. The former category includes variability in

TABLE 7–2
A Definition of Manufacturing Flexibility Grounded in Terms of Competitive Advantage

Quality-Associated Flexibility Dimensions
   Material: Ability to accommodate variation in the quality of purchased
      materials.
   Output: Ability to make products with different quality requirements.

Product-Associated Flexibility Dimensions
   New product: Ability to introduce new products.
   Modification: Ability to modify existing products.

Service-Associated Flexibility Dimensions
   Delivery: Ability to change the current production and/or delivery schedule to
      accommodate unanticipated needs.
   Volume: Ability to vary aggregate production volume from period to period.
   Mix: Ability to manufacture a variety of products within a fixed period without
      major modification of existing facilities.

Cost-Associated Flexibility Dimensions
   Factor: Ability to modify the mix of resources (materials, labor, and capital)
      used in the production process.

customer demand, vendor problems, governmental intervention, actions by competitors, and acts of nature. The latter contains machine breakdowns, absenteeism, quality problems, changes in product mix, and introduction of new processes. Organizations capable of responding to these conditions are said to possess flexibility, yet this lumps some very different capabilities under a single name. A more precise way of addressing flexibility is needed.

Table 7–2 depicts flexibility with eight dimensions.[3] The key to making this flexibility lexicon useful in a particular company is to first understand each dimension in terms of its strategic importance. Thereafter, using the strategy-actions-measures paradigm, firms can determine more precisely which kinds of flexibility are needed, what actions can lead to their attainment, and what measures are consistent with achieving them.

[3]This framework is a variant of one proposed by Donald Gerwin; see, "A Framework for Analyzing the Flexibility of Manufacturing Processes," Working Paper (Milwaukee, Wis.: School of Business Administration, University of Wisconsin-Milwaukee, 1983).

Depending on which kind of flexibility is desired, the actions will differ, as will the appropriate measures.

Material Flexibility

In some businesses, the ability to adjust to variation in the quality or characteristics of raw materials may allow one to continue producing products of superior quality, or to simply continue producing, when the competition cannot. The textile industry offers a good example of this type of flexibility. Cotton fibers differ drastically, depending on their origin, and manufacturers with the flexibility to produce consistent quality output in the face of raw material variations have an advantage.

The problem is also found in smaller degrees in other kinds of companies. Printing firms, for example, find that papers coming from different suppliers, even though of a common grade, take ink differently. A convivial example is found in the wine industry. Grapes grown even in contiguous fields can develop different characteristics. A skillful vintner can blend the grapes to produce a superior wine, while a less adept winery might produce an average bottling commanding a far lower price.

Material flexibility is needed for any factory, but in some, the relative size of the problem is less than in others. If attaining this type of flexibility is strategically important, the resultant set of actions would probably focus on manufacturing processes and on ways to anticipate when different procedures are indicated. That is, how can adaptation to the variability in inputs be most readily attained, and when will it be needed?

> The measures one might use to achieve material flexibility include changeover times, process bandwidth, settings of equipment that apply to different conditions, variances associated with processes and outputs, defect rates, detailed quality measures such as Pareto analysis metrics, and comparison of actual results with those expected for particular kinds of materials.

In all cases, the desire would be to focus on learning—at the detail levels of the company—to develop the necessary flexibility so variability in material inputs becomes a routine problem. At that point, the measures shift from strategic to maintenance, and managerial efforts can be deployed to solution of other problems.

Output Flexibility

The other type of flexibility associated with quality is the ability of a factory to produce outputs of more than one quality level. This is a classic problem, whether one is concerned with the same assembly plant making Cadillacs and Oldsmobiles, a chip manufacturer selling more than one grade of the same chip, or a restaurant catering to more than one type of clientele.

Sometimes the problem arises when demand for one product is inadequate to keep a production facility adequately utilized, and the ability to produce goods with different quality standards appears to be advantageous. This often does not work. Inducing workers who are used to producing at high quality standards to produce at lower ones is very difficult. The reverse is even more true; if something was "good enough" before, it is hard to make it not so now.

The most difficult approach to achieving output flexibility is to tie the basis for the difference in quality to labor force efforts. If this is the case, it will probably be necessary to tightly measure labor times, have differential standards, and closely monitor results—both in terms of the labor input times and the output quality levels.

If the quality output flexibility is achieved by differing material input qualities, the problem is more tractable. Here, the difference in internal cultural value will not be as severe. The same is true if the difference is somehow determined by the equipment. Perhaps some chemicals are combined in differing ways, or parts are machined to different tolerances on different kinds of equipment.

> Achieving output flexibility is fundamentally easier when differences in quality are determined by equipment or by input materials differences. The measurement problems are also less daunting.

Adherence to prescribed practices is the key, and measurements should determine that this is occurring. Also, final output measures should be directed to quality—particularly to the lower quality products to see if they are getting too good! In general, this should never be a problem, but a firm needs to continually beware of producing a low-quality (and low-price) item that competes on quality with its higher priced items.

New Product Flexibility

The ability to introduce new products rapidly, and to do so at relatively low cost, has become less a path to competitive advantage than a survival necessity for many firms. Examples of companies that have prospered through their ability to renew and add to their product portfolio, like 3M and Hewlett-Packard, are well known. Firms in the high fashion segment of the textile industry create secure niches for themselves by moving new product ideas from the conceptual stage to full production in minimal time. Japanese auto manufacturers succeeded in penetrating the U.S. market not only because their conformance quality was superior, but also because of their ability to introduce new products more rapidly than their U.S. competition.

The flip side is seen in a growing list of casualties in the North American electronics industry, where work force reductions and restructuring are an ongoing event. The underlying cause is often a lack of new products being offered to the customers.

> The drivers of increased new product flexibility include better engineering efforts, better integration between design and manufacturing engineering, and better coordination with marketing in the determination of customer needs.

In short, the actions that seem to work are those that cross an organization's functional silos with a focus on the flow of new product introduction—from conception to sale.

Actions taken to address this aspect of flexibility often include the involvement of manufacturing earlier and more deeply in the entire new product introduction cycle, the development of processes and procedures that better accommodate change, and the development of wider "bandwidth"—the ability to better respond to nonroutine events. Measurements that support new product introductions are throughput time measures for new products, comparison of actual results with plans (and analysis of underlying root causes of deviations), development of idle or nonmanufacturing time (under the whole person concept), percentage of sales comprised of products no more than X months old, achievement of project results—in all areas—and the extent to which new products require subsequent modifications and cost improvements.

Some companies are also beginning to collect measures that dissolve traditional functional boundary distinctions. They are monitoring the number of trips taken to customer locations by manufacturing personnel and the hours spent in meetings with members of other functional areas. Even budgets can be focused toward product introduction improvements when it is stipulated that a percentage of resources must be allocated to activities that integrate manufacturing with customers or other functions.

> Equally important in supporting new product introduction is elimination of measures. A focus on cost-based measures, labor utilization, machine utilization, cost reductions, reduced prices from vendors, and functionally oriented measures (that keep attention focused inside the silos) can all impede the process.

As noted in the Wang example, use of management by objectives (MBO) techniques can also detract from the overall goals. New product introduction flexibility requires a fundamental change in the culture of the firm; it is imperative to break out of restrictive practices and measures.

Modification Flexibility

The ability to modify existing products to better meet customer demands is the essence of modification flexibility. The distinction between a new product and a modification is not black and white; they represent different points on a continuum. A product is considered new when its basic functional characteristics differ from those of any product offered by the company. A modification is a product feature whose characteristics permit the basic function of the product to be accomplished in a better way.

Modification flexibility is a key strategic goal in many kinds of manufacturing companies. An example is a New England company that makes specialized word processing systems for the newspaper industry. Their value added comes from two sources: software development and integration of new software with new computing possibilities. In essence, this company understands that whenever Motorola announces a new chip, Sun Microsystems will follow with a new workstation design, and it needs to incorporate this new power into its systems and equipment.

> This firm needs to anticipate many kinds of new hardware developments, to determine what modifications are now allowed for the software, to develop the new software, to integrate all the hardware and software elements, and to do this faster than its competitors.

Another recent example of modification flexibility providing competitive advantage is found in the aircraft engine business. The quick modification of a fan for a midsize jet engine allowed GE to capture orders for the new Airbus 340 wide body. An international consortium led by Pratt & Whitney failed to move as quickly, and GE was able to garner orders worth more than $1 billion.[4]

Many of the same actions and measures that are appropriate for new product flexibility are equally relevant to modification flexibility. The primary differences relate to an approach to change. Is the issue new processes and products, or different uses of existing people, equipment, and other infrastructure?

> Achieving this kind of flexibility requires an infrastructure that supports modification flexibility. Included are the emphasis given to purchasing, engineering, and other areas to continually scan the world for developments in new technology that might permit a useful modification of existing products.

Modification flexibility can be more important than new product flexibility in some cases. The issue is one of small steps

---

[4]Russell Mitchell and Judith H. Dobrzynski, "Jack Welch: How Good a Manager?" *Business Week,* December 14, 1987, p. 95.

versus strategic leaps; both are required, and a singular focus on one will be suboptimal.

Delivery Flexibility

The ability to change the current production and/or delivery schedule is a reflection of delivery flexibility. These changes may be prompted either by outside demands, such as customer requests for rush deliveries, or by internal problems such as machine breakdowns. A good example of a firm that has recognized the strategic importance of delivery flexibility is a Northern Telecom division that maintains the ability to deliver complete switching systems to customers anywhere in the continental United States within four days, a fraction of the normal lead time for such a product (NTI has done it in less than 24 hours). Although this capacity is seldom tapped, the ability to respond to emergency needs confers multiple benefits, of which the additional business represented by the rush orders is probably the least important.

> Delivery flexibility leads to increased customer loyalty, and in some instances, the rush deliveries introduce the company's products to new customers.

The advantage of having delivery flexibility in response to machine or materials handling breakdowns is that service dependability can be maintained. The widespread adoption of JIT systems makes achievement of delivery flexibility vital. No longer can unanticipated customer needs and various versions of Murphy's Law in the factory be buffered with wads of inventory. Delivery flexibility is achieved by configuring manufacturing for responsiveness. Actions need to address ways in which the processes and the people can react to various contingencies. Whole people need to be employed, and surge capacity needs to be developed.

The measures that support delivery flexibility include those that support JIT to the extent that JIT actions are a response to the overall strategy. Included are the usual throughput, inventory turnover, and work-in-process measures. Also, measures that support development of the whole person concept and flexible use of people are important. Overall measures should include customer delivery measures and complaints. Once again, excessive focus on machine and labor utilizations is likely to be counterproductive.

Volume Flexibility

Closely related to delivery flexibility is the ability to vary aggregate output from one period to the next. This has long been considered a desirable characteristic in cyclical industries and in businesses where the sales variance is high.

> More and more firms find it exceedingly difficult to forecast demand. The answer is to configure manufacturing for response. The ultimate goal is to make anything, for anyone, anywhere, in zero lead time, with no inventories!

Accomplishing this objective totally will occur only in a few rare firms. A significant move in this direction is the essence of volume flexibility.

Measurement to support volume flexibility must focus on which measures to eliminate. Capacity simply cannot be utilized at the same level of intensity, and all measures that are so driven need to be exorcised.

Nonrepetitive applications of JIT will be required, and actions and measures that support introduction and use of these approaches are to be encouraged. Potential actions include the use of temporary employees for volume surges and partnerships with suppliers based on their volume flexibility. Possible measures of volume flexibility include inventory levels, processing times, setup times, missed sales, and variability in period-to-period output rates. Clearly, some of these reflect the results of volume flexibility, while others address its sources. Either source or result measures suffice as maintenance measures, but for improving volume flexibility, the focus needs to be on the sources.

Mix Flexibility

Mix flexibility, the ability to manufacture a variety of products in a short time, is another key type of flexibility. Aside from the potential benefits, it may confer through its contribution to delivery flexibility, mix flexibility can create competitive advantages by itself. Marketing people have said for years that a full product line yields a higher probability of sales, and there is some truth to the claim. Mix flexibility also can be thought of as insurance that aggregate volume can be maintained. Product life cycles are shorter; manufacturing a portfolio of products may assist in offsetting the effects of a decline in popularity of any particular product.

For many firms, the size of the product line continues to grow.

> The goal is to maintain a full product line (assuming that one is required by the marketplace) without high inventory and obsolescence costs.

The actions that lead to this desired result are typically JIT, clever product design based on commonality of parts and processes, good master production scheduling (MPS) design that minimizes frozen time periods and allows many changes, and manufacturing infrastructure that responds to change quickly and effectively.

The measures that support mix flexibility are all those that support the actions, such as the JIT measurements, manufacturing lead times, setup times, number of part numbers and other measures of parts standardization efforts, freeze periods and MPS performance, and the percentage of customer orders whose configuration is not known some number of weeks before shipment.

Factor Flexibility

The ability to change the mix of materials, labor, and capital used in the production process represents one view of factor flexibility. Factor flexibility has a large impact on the competitiveness of most firms in the long run. Firms that can replace labor with capital have the opportunity to reduce costs in regions or countries with relatively high labor rates. However, factor flexibility creates strategic advantages in other ways. Some textile firms have built market niches by finding products that require technologically advanced production methods that competitors in less developed nations are incapable of managing. The key is to match the competitive environment with the factors that make the most sense.

In the very long run, factor flexibility assures that a firm can keep pace with the evolution of technology. A number of U.S. firms have lost competitive advantages because of their inability to embrace the opportunities offered by computer-based systems such as CAD/CAM, CIM, and FMS. The definition of factors needs to include key technologies as well as the more usual input categories.

A manufacturing firm needs to anticipate both technological advances and the way these new factors can be integrated into its manufacturing infrastructure. Basing these questions solely on the typical capital budgeting methodologies has led to many problems.

> Achieving factor flexibility requires a mind-set: How would the manufacturing assets and organization be configured if X technology were included? What kinds of people and organizational structures are required to most easily implement new factors into the firm? How can a particular concept be implemented faster— whether it be a new piece of technology, computer software, or a new mix of offshore/onshore manufacturing?

Measurements that support attainment of factor flexibility include the average age of equipment in the factory, the yearly expenditures for new technology, the performance of projects to implement major changes in manufacturing practices, attitude surveys to test the support of employees for the directions being taken by the company, and assessments of opportunities made by consultants.

Summary of the Framework

Each of the eight dimensions of flexibility is associated with a different set of strategic objectives, different actions to achieve those objectives, and different measurements that support the strategy and the actions.

Each firm needs to clearly articulate which type of flexibility it wants to achieve. That is, what specific flexibilities are strategically important? Then a set of action programs can be designed to achieve the flexibilities, and the right group of measurements can be formulated to bolster both the actions and the strategies.

Some flexibilities require totally different kinds of actions and measurements. However, a careful review of the actions and measures indicates some are quite robust.

> JIT and its associated measures seem to be congruent with almost any dimension of flexibility.

This is helpful—but only for so long. As the company achieves JIT and asks the "what next?" question, it may find itself in a quest for more unique forms of flexibility, with attendant actions and measures.

The data generated by the PMQ confirm that managers are generally dissatisfied with the state of flexibility measurement. Consistently, managers assessed improvement in the areas of new product flexibility, mix flexibility, and factor flexibility as among the most important strategic initiatives for their companies. Just as consistently, they reported that their performance measurement systems provided far less than the average level of support for those improvements.

Conversations with managers in those firms, and in a number of other companies, show that flexibility measurement is at best an ad hoc undertaking at this time. However, there are some consistencies in the types of measures used in different companies.

> The typical measures used to track flexibility are nonfinancial. Moreover, they are partial measures, that is, they do not attempt to capture all of the elements of a flexibility dimension.

For example, one textile firm evaluates new product flexibility by looking at the turnaround time for product samples, the time elapsing from receipt of specifications to shipment of a sample. A company in a different industry tracks its mix flexibility by following the number of model numbers on the shop floor at any given time. These partial measures are not inappropriate, but the risk exists that by concentrating on only one aspect of a flexibility dimension, the true performance is not captured.

Flexibility measurement is also particularly difficult because flexibility often exists as a potential—an as yet unexpressed ability—rather than as a tangible output. Even when a type of flexibility is realized, as in the successful introduction of a new product, its characteristics often do not conform to normal accounting or performance review periods. This makes measurement doubly difficult. It does not mean, however, that the task is impossible. An organization following the design steps summarized in the next section should be able to develop adequate, although probably not perfect, measures of flexibility.

MEASUREMENT DESIGN FOR THE NEW COMPETITIVE PRIORITIES

It seems appropriate to conclude by reviewing the elements in the design of a measurement system suitable for the newly emerging competitive priorities. The two key design elements are the process by which measures are selected and the objectives against which they can be judged.

The Measurement System Design Process

A company that has truly embraced change has in place a mechanism for triggering a review of its measurement system. Ideally, this happens whenever a change leads to disequilibrium in the strategy, actions, and measures. More realistically, the review is conducted periodically. It is logically associated with the strategy formulation process.

The measurement review is done by a task team, comprised of management from the levels in the organization that use and are evaluated by the measures in question. Staff can design the process for the team to follow, but only line managers can make it work. The group should be large enough to encompass all of the functions affected by the measures, although for effectiveness, smaller is better.

The cross-functional composition of the team should be emphasized, particularly given the nature of activities associated with the new priorities. Many of the new competitive priorities, such as quality, new product introduction, customer service, and overhead deployment, are focused on upstream and downstream activities. They cross organizational silos. Consequently, cross-functional input is essential.

Once the team is formed, the process is top-down, bottom-up. This means the strategy has to be clearly articulated. In some instances, this may require that the team invest time in conducting a full-blown competitive analysis. In other situations, it may be as simple as adopting a previously written mission statement. Whatever the case, the team needs to attain a clear understanding of its organization's role in supporting the business strategy, with a particular emphasis on customer needs and expectations. From this analysis, the team should identify the critical success factors, the drivers, for the unit.

The bottom-up phase of the process consists of the actual creation of the new measurement system. Depending on the nature of the strategic and environmental changes that have occurred since the last measurement review, the process may be directed as much toward the deletion of measures as it is to addition of new measures. This depends on the movement between strategic and maintenance categories.

Identification of new measures is ordinarily straightforward, assuming the analytical groundwork has been carefully done. With some of the new competitive priorities, it is not easy to find individual measures that capture all the dimensions of interest, as discussed in the section on flexibility, but adequate metrics can be developed so long as it is remembered that direction, not precision, is the key. Taking an experimental point of view is useful, too. Try a measure for a period, assess its effectiveness, and change it or eliminate it depending on the results.

Every team is going to develop a set of measures oriented to its unit's unique mix of history, strategy, technology, and organizational culture. However, this does not say the resultant system does not need to meet certain criteria to be deemed suitable.

Attributes of Good Measurement Systems[5]

Regardless of which competitive priorities companies pursue, the successful measurement systems will share five characteristics. Measurement systems should:

1. Be mutually supportive and consistent with the business's operating goals, objectives, critical success factors, and programs.
2. Convey information through as few and as simple a set of measures as possible.
3. Reveal how effectively customers' needs and expectations are satisfied. Focus on measures that customers can see.
4. Provide a set of measurements for each organizational component that allows all members of the organization to understand how their decisions and activities affect the entire business.
5. Support organizational learning and continuous improvement.

The first characteristic represents the intersection of the three-phase change model and the strategy-actions-measures model.

> Maintaining consistency between an organization's strategy, actions, and measures is the essence of embracing change.

The adoption of any new competitive priority necessitates a review of the match between strategy, actions, and measures that almost surely will dictate some changes in the measurement system. The challenge facing managers is to identify a mechanism that will assure these reviews are triggered whenever conditions change.

---

[5]More information on some of the ideas presented in this section may be found in a paper by one of our colleagues, Duncan McDougall, "Learning the Ropes: How to Tell When You've Found an Effective Measurement System for Manufacturing," Boston University Manufacturing Roundtable Working Paper, 1988.

The second characteristic harks back to the earlier discussion of strategic and maintenance measures and of deleting old measures. Information has value only if it can be effectively processed.

> Companies should strive to have enough measures to solve problems, but avoid collecting data that will only create confusion.

When measures are no longer strategically relevant, they should be eliminated.

Keeping measures focused on the customer is a path to manufacturing excellence and to competitive strength. Customer expectations are satisfied by performance on factors like quality, delivery times, and responsiveness to special needs.

> Attending to internal factors such as cost or productivity is not necessarily inconsistent with customer satisfaction, but it does not assure that customers' needs will be addressed.

By concentrating on those things that customers can see, the organization strengthens its competitive position. Virtually all of the new competitive priorities are customer-oriented. Consequently, a measurement system designed to support the new competitive priorities should lead to an enhanced competitive position.

Measures should be operative at a basic level in manufacturing, not just in some overall aggregate that will have only an indirect impact on day-to-day activity.

> At every level in the organization, measures should enable people to assess their own performance; moreover, the goal should be for every person to understand how their actions support or inhibit achievement of the company's strategic objectives.

An effective top-down, bottom-up measurement change process contributes to accomplishing this. When lower level managers, supervisors, and workers identify appropriate measures based on the strategic vision communicated from top management, they understand not only the measures, but also how the performance represented by those measures affects the competitive health of the company.

Finally, a good measurement system *must* support organizational learning and continuous improvement.

"What next?" is not a one-time question.

The company that is ready, willing, and able to answer it most often, the company that has learned to meet the performance measurement challenge and embrace change, that company will be the winner in the race for competitive supremacy.

APPENDIX A
BOSTON UNIVERSITY MANUFACTURING
ROUNDTABLE PERFORMANCE
MEASUREMENT RESEARCH PROJECT

This questionnaire is part of a research project investigating manufacturing performance measurement which is being conducted by the Boston University Manufacturing Roundtable. The purpose of this questionnaire is to gather data about the approaches to manufacturing performance measurement used by manufacturers on the leading edge of production methodology. Your help will be greatly appreciated. Your responses are to be anonymous; please do not put your name anywhere in this booklet. Please answer all the questions as frankly as possible.

PART I
Respondent/Organizational Unit Profile

This questionnaire is being administered to many managers in your company. For classification purposes, please provide the following information.

1) What is the name of the organizational unit for which you are responding?

_____

2) Please ask the person who is administering this questionnaire to inform you as to which group your organizational unit falls into, and then check the appropriate box.

Group I .... [　]
Group II .... [　]
Group III .... [　]

3) Please check the box for the one functional responsibility area below which BEST describes the nature of your primary activity.
[　] Manufacturing line management
[　] Other manufacturing-related management (e.g., quality, materials)

[   ] Finance/Accounting management
[   ] Sales/marketing management
[   ] Engineering management

General Instructions

The questions in this booklet ask you to give your opinions on performance measurement for *production*. You are asked to answer all questions, leaving none blank. If you cannot determine an answer for a particular question, please mark "DK" for "don't know" in the margin next to the item.

PART II
Production Improvement

Left-Hand Scale

The following list presents areas in which many companies are trying to improve manufacturing effectiveness. For each of these areas, circle the number on the *left-hand scale* that indicates your opinion of the relative degree of importance that *improvement* in this area has for the long-run health of your company. If you feel that improvement in the area is of little or no importance to your company, you should circle the "1" on the left-hand scale for that item. If you believe, on the other hand, that improvement in the named area is of very great importance to your company's long-term health, you should circle the "7." When your opinion is that the item is somewhere between the two extremes, you should circle the number that reflects its relative position.

Right-Hand Scale

On the *right-hand scale,* circle the number that corresponds to the extent to which you feel current company performance measures support or inhibit improvement in each of these areas.

EXAMPLE: The first area for which you are asked to provide ratings on importance and support for improvement is quality. If you believe that additional improvement in the quality of products is extremely important, you should circle 7 on the left-hand scale. If, however, you believe that further improvement in quality is of little importance (that is, that current quality must be maintained, but that improvement is not at all critical), you should circle 1 on the left scale. Similarly, if you believe that current performance measures strongly encourage improvement in quality, you should circle 7 on the right-hand scale. If these measures work against improvement in quality, circle 1 on the right-hand scale.

Performance Measurement Questionnaire

IMPROVEMENT AREAS	Long-Run Importance of Improvement None >>>>> Great	Effect of Current Performance Measures on Improvement Inhibit >> Support
QUALITY	1 2 3 4 5 6 7	1 2 3 4 5 6 7
LABOR EFFICIENCY	1 2 3 4 5 6 7	1 2 3 4 5 6 7
MACHINE EFFICIENCY	1 2 3 4 5 6 7	1 2 3 4 5 6 7
NEW PRODUCT INTRODUCTION	1 2 3 4 5 6 7	1 2 3 4 5 6 7
VOLUME FLEXIBILITY	1 2 3 4 5 6 7	1 2 3 4 5 6 7
PRODUCT MIX FLEXIBILITY	1 2 3 4 5 6 7	1 2 3 4 5 6 7
PRODUCT TECHNOLOGY	1 2 3 4 5 6 7	1 2 3 4 5 6 7
PROCESS TECHNOLOGY	1 2 3 4 5 6 7	1 2 3 4 5 6 7
MANUFACTURING THROUGHPUT TIMES	1 2 3 4 5 6 7	1 2 3 4 5 6 7

	1	2	3	4	5	6	7		1	2	3	4	5	6	7
INTEGRATION WITH SUPPLIERS	1	2	3	4	5	6	7		1	2	3	4	5	6	7
INTEGRATION WITH CUSTOMERS	1	2	3	4	5	6	7		1	2	3	4	5	6	7
INFORMATION SYSTEMS	1	2	3	4	5	6	7		1	2	3	4	5	6	7
DIRECT COST REDUCTION	1	2	3	4	5	6	7		1	2	3	4	5	6	7
OVERHEAD COST REDUCTION	1	2	3	4	5	6	7		1	2	3	4	5	6	7
INVENTORY MANAGEMENT	1	2	3	4	5	6	7		1	2	3	4	5	6	7
JOB RESPONSIBILITIES	1	2	3	4	5	6	7		1	2	3	4	5	6	7
PERFORMANCE MEASUREMENT	1	2	3	4	5	6	7		1	2	3	4	5	6	7
CUSTOMER SATISFACTION	1	2	3	4	5	6	7		1	2	3	4	5	6	7
ENVIRONMENTAL CONTROL	1	2	3	4	5	6	7		1	2	3	4	5	6	7
MANUFACTURING STRATEGY	1	2	3	4	5	6	7		1	2	3	4	5	6	7
PROCUREMENT PRACTICES	1	2	3	4	5	6	7		1	2	3	4	5	6	7
OFFSHORE MANUFACTURING	1	2	3	4	5	6	7		1	2	3	4	5	6	7
COMPUTER INTEGRATED MANUFACTURING (CIM)	1	2	3	4	5	6	7		1	2	3	4	5	6	7
EDUCATION AND TRAINING	1	2	3	4	5	6	7		1	2	3	4	5	6	7

PART III
Performance Factors

Left-Hand Scale

The following list presents factors by which many companies attempt to evaluate their performance. For each of these manufacturing "performance factors," circle the number on the left-hand scale that indicates your assessment of how important achieving excellence in this factor is for the long-run health of the company.

Right-Hand Scale

On the right-hand scale, circle the number that corresponds to the extent to which you feel the company presently emphasizes measurement of each performance factor.

EXAMPLE: The first area for which you are asked to provide ratings on importance and emphasis of performance factors is inventory turnover. If you believe that inventory turnover is an extremely important factor, you should circle 7 on the left-hand scale. If, however, you believe that inventory turnover is of little importance to your company (that is, it is a factor that may be ignored in the success of your company), you should circle 1 on the left-hand scale. Similarly, if you believe that inventory turnover is strongly *emphasized in measuring performance,* you should circle a high number on the right-hand scale (a "7," for example). If this measure is *virtually ignored,* circle a low number on the right-hand scale (a "1," for example).

Performance Measurement Questionnaire

Importance of Performance Factor None >>>>> Great	PERFORMANCE FACTORS	Company's Emphasis on Measurement None >>>>> Major
1 2 3 4 5 6 7	INVENTORY TURNOVER	1 2 3 4 5 6 7
1 2 3 4 5 6 7	CONFORMANCE TO SPECIFICATIONS	1 2 3 4 5 6 7
1 2 3 4 5 6 7	COST OF QUALITY	1 2 3 4 5 6 7
1 2 3 4 5 6 7	MANUFACTURING LEAD TIMES	1 2 3 4 5 6 7
1 2 3 4 5 6 7	VENDOR QUALITY	1 2 3 4 5 6 7
1 2 3 4 5 6 7	VENDOR LEAD TIMES	1 2 3 4 5 6 7
1 2 3 4 5 6 7	DIRECT LABOR PRODUCTIVITY	1 2 3 4 5 6 7
1 2 3 4 5 6 7	INDIRECT LABOR PRODUCTIVITY	1 2 3 4 5 6 7
1 2 3 4 5 6 7	CHANGEOVER/SETUP TIMES	1 2 3 4 5 6 7
1 2 3 4 5 6 7	SALES FORECAST ACCURACY	1 2 3 4 5 6 7
1 2 3 4 5 6 7	NUMBER OF ENGINEERING CHANGES	1 2 3 4 5 6 7
1 2 3 4 5 6 7	EDUCATION/TRAINING BUDGETS	1 2 3 4 5 6 7
1 2 3 4 5 6 7	RECORD ACCURACY	1 2 3 4 5 6 7
1 2 3 4 5 6 7	ON-TIME DELIVERY	1 2 3 4 5 6 7
1 2 3 4 5 6 7	CUSTOMER SURVEYS	1 2 3 4 5 6 7
1 2 3 4 5 6 7	NUMBER OF SUPPLIERS	1 2 3 4 5 6 7
1 2 3 4 5 6 7	NUMBER OF MATERIAL PART NUMBERS	1 2 3 4 5 6 7
1 2 3 4 5 6 7	CAPACITY UTILIZATION	1 2 3 4 5 6 7
1 2 3 4 5 6 7	MEETING PRODUCTION SCHEDULES	1 2 3 4 5 6 7
1 2 3 4 5 6 7	COST REDUCTION: DOLLAR SAVINGS	1 2 3 4 5 6 7
1 2 3 4 5 6 7	DOLLARS OF CAPITAL INVESTMENT	1 2 3 4 5 6 7
1 2 3 4 5 6 7	PROCESS R & D COSTS	1 2 3 4 5 6 7

PERFORMANCE FACTORS
(continued)

Importance of Performance Factor (None >>>>> Great)	Performance Factor	Company's Emphasis on Measurement (None >>>>> Major)
1 2 3 4 5 6 7	PRODUCT R & D COSTS	1 2 3 4 5 6 7
1 2 3 4 5 6 7	SAFETY	1 2 3 4 5 6 7
1 2 3 4 5 6 7	NEW PRODUCT INTRODUCTION	1 2 3 4 5 6 7
1 2 3 4 5 6 7	NEW MODEL INTRODUCTION	1 2 3 4 5 6 7
1 2 3 4 5 6 7	DOLLAR SHIPMENTS PER PERIOD	1 2 3 4 5 6 7
1 2 3 4 5 6 7	NEW PROCESS/EQUIPMENT INTRODUCTIONS	1 2 3 4 5 6 7
1 2 3 4 5 6 7	UNIT MATERIAL COSTS	1 2 3 4 5 6 7
1 2 3 4 5 6 7	UNIT LABOR COSTS	1 2 3 4 5 6 7
1 2 3 4 5 6 7	UNIT OVERHEAD COSTS	1 2 3 4 5 6 7
1 2 3 4 5 6 7	VARIANCES	1 2 3 4 5 6 7
1 2 3 4 5 6 7	RETURN ON INVESTMENT	1 2 3 4 5 6 7
1 2 3 4 5 6 7	MARGINS (CONTRIBUTION/GROSS)	1 2 3 4 5 6 7
1 2 3 4 5 6 7	DEPARTMENT BUDGET CONTROL	1 2 3 4 5 6 7
1 2 3 4 5 6 7	YIELDS	1 2 3 4 5 6 7
1 2 3 4 5 6 7	MEETING PROJECT MILESTONES	1 2 3 4 5 6 7
1 2 3 4 5 6 7	MINIMIZING ENVIRONMENTAL WASTE	1 2 3 4 5 6 7
1 2 3 4 5 6 7	ENVIRONMENTAL MONITORING	1 2 3 4 5 6 7
1 2 3 4 5 6 7	OTHER: _____	1 2 3 4 5 6 7
1 2 3 4 5 6 7	OTHER: _____	1 2 3 4 5 6 7
1 2 3 4 5 6 7	OTHER: _____	1 2 3 4 5 6 7

PART IV
Your Performance Measures

Choose the one factor that best describes how you feel your personal performance is evaluated in each of the following five time frames. If your responsibility is in the production area, please use one of the performance factors listed in the previous section. If your primary responsibility is in another area, and none of the factors listed above is appropriate, use your own description.

1. Daily _____

2. Weekly _____

3. Monthly _____

4. Quarterly _____

5. Annually _____

Any Comments?

Thank you for your cooperation.
Please return the questionnaire to the person
from whom you received it.

APPENDIX B
BOSTON UNIVERSITY/NORTHERN TELECOM
PERFORMANCE MEASUREMENT
RESEARCH PROJECT

This questionnaire is part of a research project being conducted by Boston University investigating performance measurement. It builds upon an earlier study conducted within manufacturing plants at NTI. The purpose of this questionnaire is to gather data on perceptions of marketing performance measurement at NTI with the eventual goal of developing the best set of performance measures possible. Your help will be greatly appreciated. Your responses will remain anonymous; please do not put your name anywhere in this booklet. Please respond to all of the questions. Be as frank as possible.

PART I
Respondent/Organizational Unit Profile

This questionnaire is being administered to many marketing managers at NTI. For classification purposes, please provide the following information.

1) What is the name of the organizational unit for which you are responding?

Premier Accounts   [ ]
Federal Systems   [ ]

2) Please check the box for the one functional responsibility area below which best describes the nature of your primary activity.
[ ] Regional Vice President/Director
[ ] National Account Manager
[ ] System Engineering
[ ] Program Management
[ ] Marketing Support

General Instructions

There are four sections to this questionnaire. You have already completed the first part. The remaining questions in this booklet ask you to give your opinions on performance measurement for marketing. Please respond from your own point of view. You are asked to answer all questions, leaving none blank. If you cannot determine an answer for a particular question, please mark "DK" for "don't know" in the margin next to the item.

In each of Parts II and III, a list of items appears down the center of the page, flanked by a sequence of numbers from 1 to 7 on the left side of the page and a similar sequence on the right side. An example appears below.

1 2 3 4 5 6 7   RELIABILITY OF PRODUCTS IN FIELD   1 2 3 4 5 6 7

Each list of numbers represents a question and requires a response. Thus, there are two questions for each item. You are to circle a number in each group that represents your opinion on the question. The left-side question and the right-side question each remain constant for the whole list in that part of the booklet.

For PART II the questions are:

> LEFT SIDE: In your opinion, how much *improvement* is needed in this area for NTI's long-run success?

> RIGHT SIDE: In your opinion, does the way performance is currently measured inhibit or support improvement in this area?

For PART III, the questions are:

> LEFT SIDE: In your opinion, how *important* is performance on this factor?

> RIGHT SIDE: How much emphasis is currently placed on *measuring* this factor?

More detailed instructions are given for each part.

PART II
Performance Improvement Areas

Left-Hand Scale

The list in Part II presents areas in which many companies are trying to improve marketing effectiveness. For each of these areas, circle the number on the *left-hand scale* that indicates your opinion of the relative degree of *improvement* in this area that is required for the long-run health of Northern Telecom. If you feel that no improvement in the area is needed at NTI, you should circle the "1" on the left-hand scale for that item. If you believe, on the other hand, that much improvement in the named area is needed for NTI's long-term health, you should circle the "7." When your opinion is that the item is somewhere between the two extremes, you should circle the number that reflects its relative position.

Right-Hand Scale

On the *right-hand scale,* you should circle the number that indicates the extent to which you feel current company performance measures support or inhibit improvement in each of these areas.

LEFT SIDE: In your opinion, how much *improvement* is needed in this area for NTI's long-run success?

RIGHT SIDE: In your opinion, does the way performance is currently measured inhibit or support improvement in this area?

EXAMPLE: The first area for which you are asked to provide ratings is RELIABILITY OF PRODUCTS IN THE FIELD. On the left-hand scale, you should choose the rating that shows the amount of improvement in product reliability you think is required, regardless of your opinion of the importance of current product reliability. Speaking hypothetically, assume your opinion is that product reliability is an important product characteristic and will continue to be. However, you feel that NTI's products are extremely reliable and that *improvement* in reliability will not yield any competitive advantage, although current reliability must be maintained. Under this scenario, you should circle a low number ("1," for example) on the left-hand scale. On the right, if you felt that the entire set of performance measures for marketing strongly encourage *improvement* in product reliability, you would circle a high number ("7," for example).

Performance Measurement Questionnaire

How Much Long-Run Improvement Is Required? None >>>>> Great	IMPROVEMENT AREAS	Do Current Performance Measures Support Improvement? Inhibit >> Support
1 2 3 4 5 6 7	RELIABILITY OF PRODUCTS IN FIELD	1 2 3 4 5 6 7
1 2 3 4 5 6 7	COMPETITIVENESS OF NTI PRICES	1 2 3 4 5 6 7
1 2 3 4 5 6 7	COMPETITIVENESS OF NTI HARDWARE PERFORMANCE	1 2 3 4 5 6 7
1 2 3 4 5 6 7	COMPETITIVENESS OF NTI SOFTWARE PERFORMANCE	1 2 3 4 5 6 7
1 2 3 4 5 6 7	ABILITY OF NTI PRODUCTS TO PROVIDE NETWORK SOLUTION	1 2 3 4 5 6 7
1 2 3 4 5 6 7	ABILITY TO MEET PROMISED DELIVERY DATES	1 2 3 4 5 6 7
1 2 3 4 5 6 7	ABILITY TO SATISFY CUSTOMER REQUESTS	1 2 3 4 5 6 7
1 2 3 4 5 6 7	COMMISSION TRACKING & REPORTING PROCEDURES	1 2 3 4 5 6 7
1 2 3 4 5 6 7	CUSTOMER INSTALLED BASE INFORMATION SYSTEM	1 2 3 4 5 6 7
1 2 3 4 5 6 7	PRODUCT TECHNICAL DATA AVAILABILITY	1 2 3 4 5 6 7
1 2 3 4 5 6 7	CONSISTENCY OF QUALITY OF SUPPORT PROVIDED BY NTI PRODUCT DIVISIONS	1 2 3 4 5 6 7
1 2 3 4 5 6 7	CONSISTENCY OF QUALITY OF SUPPORT PROVIDED BY BNR	1 2 3 4 5 6 7
1 2 3 4 5 6 7	COMMON UNDERSTANDING OF MARKETING STRATEGY	1 2 3 4 5 6 7
1 2 3 4 5 6 7	MESH BETWEEN MARKETING STRATEGY AND OPERATIONS STRATEGY	1 2 3 4 5 6 7

IMPROVEMENT AREAS (continued)	How Much Long-Run Improvement Is Required? None >>>>> Great	Do Current Performance Measures Support Improvement? Inhibit >> Support
MESH BETWEEN MARKETING STRATEGY AND CORPORATE STRATEGY	1 2 3 4 5 6 7	1 2 3 4 5 6 7
QUALITY OF PRODUCT EDUCATION AND TRAINING	1 2 3 4 5 6 7	1 2 3 4 5 6 7
EQUITY OF MFA PERFORMANCE MEASURES	1 2 3 4 5 6 7	1 2 3 4 5 6 7
EQUITY OF SALES INCENTIVES AND REWARDS	1 2 3 4 5 6 7	1 2 3 4 5 6 7
EFFECTIVENESS OF ADVERTISING AND PROMOTION	1 2 3 4 5 6 7	1 2 3 4 5 6 7
COMMON UNDERSTANDING OF NT NETWORKING STRATEGY	1 2 3 4 5 6 7	1 2 3 4 5 6 7
QUALITY OF AFTER-SALES SERVICE TO END USERS	1 2 3 4 5 6 7	1 2 3 4 5 6 7
ACCURACY OF FORECASTS	1 2 3 4 5 6 7	1 2 3 4 5 6 7
FORECAST REPORTING REQUIREMENTS	1 2 3 4 5 6 7	1 2 3 4 5 6 7
ABILITY TO ACT AS SYSTEMS INTEGRATOR	1 2 3 4 5 6 7	1 2 3 4 5 6 7
JOINT CUSTOMER-NTI ACCOUNT PLANNING	1 2 3 4 5 6 7	1 2 3 4 5 6 7
ACCOUNT PLAN DOCUMENTATION	1 2 3 4 5 6 7	1 2 3 4 5 6 7
CUSTOMER RELATIONSHIP BUILDING	1 2 3 4 5 6 7	1 2 3 4 5 6 7
USE OF NTI EXECUTIVES WITHIN ACCOUNTS	1 2 3 4 5 6 7	1 2 3 4 5 6 7
NAM'S KNOWLEDGE OF PRODUCT TECHNICAL DATA	1 2 3 4 5 6 7	1 2 3 4 5 6 7

Item	Rating
NAM'S KNOWLEDGE OF PRODUCT APPLICATIONS	1 2 3 4 5 6 7
INSTITUTE FOR INFORMATION STUDIES	1 2 3 4 5 6 7
QUOTA SETTING PROCESS	1 2 3 4 5 6 7
QUOTA ACHIEVEMENT	1 2 3 4 5 6 7
NEW PRODUCT COMMUNICATION TO CUSTOMERS	1 2 3 4 5 6 7
INTERNAL COMMUNICATION OF NEW PRODUCT INFORMATION	1 2 3 4 5 6 7
EFFECTIVE USE OF CUSTOMER INPUT INTO PRODUCT DEVELOPMENT	1 2 3 4 5 6 7
SALES EXPENSE CONTROL	1 2 3 4 5 6 7
DISTRIBUTOR RELATIONSHIP BUILDING	1 2 3 4 5 6 7
PRODUCT DIVISIONS RELATIONSHIP BUILDING	1 2 3 4 5 6 7
GLOBAL ACCOUNT MANAGEMENT	1 2 3 4 5 6 7
POWER MARKETING	1 2 3 4 5 6 7
GLOBAL NETWORKS	1 2 3 4 5 6 7
PERSONAL/PROFESSIONAL DEVELOPMENT OPPORTUNITIES	1 2 3 4 5 6 7
PRODUCT FOCUS TO MEET CUSTOMER NEEDS	1 2 3 4 5 6 7
BILLING SYSTEMS	1 2 3 4 5 6 7
END USER SATISFACTION WITH NT DOCUMENTATION	1 2 3 4 5 6 7
CONTRACT ADMINISTRATION	1 2 3 4 5 6 7

IMPROVEMENT AREAS
(concluded)

How Much Long-Run Improvement Is Required? None >>>>> Great	Improvement Areas	Do Current Performance Measures Support Improvement? Inhibit >> Support
1 2 3 4 5 6 7	NATIONAL MASTER ORDER AGREEMENTS	1 2 3 4 5 6 7
1 2 3 4 5 6 7	GLOBAL MASTER ORDER AGREEMENTS	1 2 3 4 5 6 7
1 2 3 4 5 6 7	CUSTOMER EASE OF DOING BUSINESS WITH NTI	1 2 3 4 5 6 7
1 2 3 4 5 6 7	CONTRACT SIMPLIFICATION	1 2 3 4 5 6 7
1 2 3 4 5 6 7	ACCOUNT PLAN CONTENT	1 2 3 4 5 6 7
1 2 3 4 5 6 7	ACCOUNT PLAN UPDATING	1 2 3 4 5 6 7
1 2 3 4 5 6 7	ACCOUNT PLAN REVIEW PROCESS	1 2 3 4 5 6 7
1 2 3 4 5 6 7	NTI COMMUNITY/PROFESSIONAL INVOLVEMENT	1 2 3 4 5 6 7
1 2 3 4 5 6 7	MFA MEASUREMENT PROCESS	1 2 3 4 5 6 7

PART III
Performance Factors

Left-Hand Scale

The following list presents some factors against which various companies attempt to evaluate marketing performance. For each of these marketing "performance factors," circle the number on the *left-hand scale* that indicates your assessment of how important performance measured against this factor is to NTI.

Right-Hand Scale

On the *right-hand scale,* circle the number that corresponds to the extent to which you feel the company presently emphasizes measurement of this performance factor.

LEFT SIDE: In your opinion, how *important* is performance on this factor?

RIGHT SIDE: How much emphasis is currently placed on *measuring* this factor?

EXAMPLE: The first area for which you are asked to provide ratings on importance and emphasis of performance factors is SALES GROWTH RATE: PER ACCOUNT. If you believe that sales growth rate per account is extremely *important to NTI,* you should circle a high number on the left-hand scale (a "7," for example). If, however, you believe that achievement measured by this factor is not, in itself, important to NTI's long-term success, you should circle a low number on the left scale (a "1," for example). Similarly, if you believe that sales growth rate per account is strongly *emphasized in measuring performance in marketing at NTI,* you should circle a high number on the right-hand scale. If this measure is virtually ignored, circle a low number on the right-hand scale.

Performance Measurement Questionnaire

Of How Much Importance Is This Performance Factor? None >>>>>> Great	PERFORMANCE FACTORS	How Much Emphasis Is Currently Placed on Measuring Factor? None >>>>>> Great
1 2 3 4 5 6 7	SALES GROWTH RATE: PER ACCOUNT	1 2 3 4 5 6 7
1 2 3 4 5 6 7	SALES GROWTH RATE: PER PRODUCT	1 2 3 4 5 6 7
1 2 3 4 5 6 7	NTI'S OVERALL MARKET SHARE	1 2 3 4 5 6 7
1 2 3 4 5 6 7	NTI'S MARKET SHARE BY INDIVIDUAL ACCOUNT	1 2 3 4 5 6 7
1 2 3 4 5 6 7	ACCOUNT REVENUES: ACTUAL VS. QUOTA	1 2 3 4 5 6 7
1 2 3 4 5 6 7	REGIONAL REVENUES: ACTUAL VS. QUOTA	1 2 3 4 5 6 7
1 2 3 4 5 6 7	CUSTOMER SATISFACTION: SURVEY RATINGS	1 2 3 4 5 6 7
1 2 3 4 5 6 7	CUSTOMER SATISFACTION: DIRECT FEEDBACK	1 2 3 4 5 6 7
1 2 3 4 5 6 7	SALES GROWTH RATE OVER LAST 12 MONTHS	1 2 3 4 5 6 7
1 2 3 4 5 6 7	SALES FORECAST ACCURACY: ACTUAL VS. FORECAST	1 2 3 4 5 6 7
1 2 3 4 5 6 7	EDUCATION/TRAINING BUDGET: ACTUAL VS. BUDGET	1 2 3 4 5 6 7
1 2 3 4 5 6 7	TRAVEL AND ENTERTAINMENT EXPENSE: ACTUAL VS. BUDGET	1 2 3 4 5 6 7
1 2 3 4 5 6 7	REGION EXPENSE RATIO: DOLLAR EXPENSES DIVIDED BY DOLLAR SALES	1 2 3 4 5 6 7
1 2 3 4 5 6 7	ACCOUNT EXPENSE RATIO: DOLLAR EXPENSES DIVIDED BY DOLLAR SALES	1 2 3 4 5 6 7

REGION EXPENSE: ACTUAL VS. BUDGET	1 2 3 4 5 6 7							1 2 3 4 5 6 7						
ELAPSED TIME: ORDER TO DELIVERY	1 2 3 4 5 6 7							1 2 3 4 5 6 7						
QUARTERLY ACCOUNT STATUS REVIEW	1 2 3 4 5 6 7							1 2 3 4 5 6 7						
DELIVERY DATES: ACTUAL VS. COMMITMENT	1 2 3 4 5 6 7							1 2 3 4 5 6 7						
CONTRIBUTION MARGIN BY ACCOUNT	1 2 3 4 5 6 7							1 2 3 4 5 6 7						
NUMBER OF SALES CALLS	1 2 3 4 5 6 7							1 2 3 4 5 6 7						
RESPONSE TIME BY NAM TO CUSTOMER INQUIRIES	1 2 3 4 5 6 7							1 2 3 4 5 6 7						
PERCENTAGE OF ISDN LINES SHIPPED	1 2 3 4 5 6 7							1 2 3 4 5 6 7						
PERCENTAGE OF DATA LINES SHIPPED	1 2 3 4 5 6 7							1 2 3 4 5 6 7						
PERCENTAGE OF PROPRIETARY SETS SHIPPED PER SWITCH	1 2 3 4 5 6 7							1 2 3 4 5 6 7						
PERCENTAGE OF DIGITAL SETS SHIPPED PER SWITCH	1 2 3 4 5 6 7							1 2 3 4 5 6 7						
DISTRIBUTOR RELATIONSHIP BUILDING	1 2 3 4 5 6 7							1 2 3 4 5 6 7						
PRODUCT DIVISION RELATIONSHIP BUILDING	1 2 3 4 5 6 7							1 2 3 4 5 6 7						
CUSTOMER RELATIONSHIP BUILDING	1 2 3 4 5 6 7							1 2 3 4 5 6 7						
EFFECTIVE EXECUTIVE POSITIONING IN SUPPORT OF SALES ACTIVITIES	1 2 3 4 5 6 7							1 2 3 4 5 6 7						
WIN-LOSS REPORTS	1 2 3 4 5 6 7							1 2 3 4 5 6 7						
MEETING REPORTING DEADLINES	1 2 3 4 5 6 7							1 2 3 4 5 6 7						
QUALITY OF MONTHLY REPORTS	1 2 3 4 5 6 7							1 2 3 4 5 6 7						
ADD-ONS TO INSTALLED BASE	1 2 3 4 5 6 7							1 2 3 4 5 6 7						
EFFECTIVE USE OF CUSTOMER INPUT INTO PRODUCT DEVELOPMENT	1 2 3 4 5 6 7							1 2 3 4 5 6 7						

Of How Much Importance Is This Performance Factor? None >>>>> Great	PERFORMANCE FACTORS (*concluded*)	How Much Emphasis Is Currently Placed on Measuring Factor? None >>>>> Great
1 2 3 4 5 6 7	NEW PRODUCT MARKETING	1 2 3 4 5 6 7
1 2 3 4 5 6 7	ACCOUNT PLAN PREPARATION	1 2 3 4 5 6 7
1 2 3 4 5 6 7	ACCOUNT PLAN APPROVAL	1 2 3 4 5 6 7
1 2 3 4 5 6 7	NTI COMMUNITY/PROFESSIONAL INVOLVEMENT	1 2 3 4 5 6 7
1 2 3 4 5 6 7	QUALITY OF TECHNICAL SUPPORT PROVIDED BY PRODUCT DIVISIONS	1 2 3 4 5 6 7
1 2 3 4 5 6 7	PRODUCT, PRESENCE, AND HIT RATE (PPH)	1 2 3 4 5 6 7
1 2 3 4 5 6 7	REGIONAL SPENDING PER EMPLOYEE	1 2 3 4 5 6 7
1 2 3 4 5 6 7	REGIONAL REVENUES PER EMPLOYEE	1 2 3 4 5 6 7

PART IV
Your Performance Factors

For each of the time frames listed below, choose the primary factor or factors that best describe how *your* personal performance is evaluated. Use your own words, but try to provide clear descriptions.

1. Daily
2. Weekly
3. Monthly
4. Quarterly
5. Annually

Any Comments?

Thank you for your cooperation.

INDEX